Great
Horse Treks
of the World

Great Horse Treks

NEW HOLLAND

of the World   *By* JULIE MILLER

NEW
HOLLAND

First published in 2004 by
New Holland Publishers
London • Cape Town • Sydney • Auckland
www.newhollandpublishers.com

86 Edgware Road
London W2 2EA
United Kingdom

80 McKenzie Street
Cape Town 8001
South Africa

14 Aquatic Drive
Frenchs Forest, NSW 2086
Australia

218 Lake Road
Northcote, Auckland
New Zealand

ISBN 1 84330 725 1

PUBLISHER Mariëlle Renssen
PUBLISHING MANAGERS Claudia dos Santos, Simon Pooley
COMMISSIONING EDITOR Alfred LeMaitre
EDITOR Leizel Brown
DESIGNER Peter Bosman
CARTOGRAPHY Nicole Engeler
PICTURE RESEARCH Karla Kik
PROOFREADER Anna Tanneberger
PRODUCTION Myrna Collins

REPRODUCTION BY
Hirt & Carter (Cape) Pty Ltd
PRINTED AND BOUND IN SINGAPORE BY
Tien Wah Press (Pte) Ltd

2 4 6 8 10 9 7 5 3 1

HALF TITLE *The Mongolian horse is a product of
its landscape – tough and free-spirited.*

TITLE *The challenge of navigation in the Pennines of northern England.*

ABOVE *Trail riding, Western style, on a dude ranch in Wyoming.*

OVERLEAF *A group of riders crosses a shallow river in the Waterberg region of South Africa.*

Contents

Introduction   8

The Americas   12

CANADA
Canadian Rockies Grandeur   14

USA
Bitterroot Roundup   20

MEXICO
Cavalcade de Bravo   28

COSTA RICA
From Pacific Beach to Cloud Forest   34

CHILE
Torres Del Paine Vistas   40

Europe   46

ICELAND
Glaciers and Deserts of Iceland   48

IRELAND
Discovering Sligo on Horseback   54

SCOTLAND
The Argyll Highlands   60

ENGLAND
Exploring England on Horseback   66

FRANCE
Exploring the Camargue   74

SPAIN
The Forests and Beaches of Andalucia   80

ITALY
Bridle Trails of Umbria   88

HUNGARY
Csikós of the Puszta — 94

TURKEY
Land of Beautiful Horses — 102

Africa — 108

SOUTH AFRICA
Waterberg Wilderness Adventure — 110

BOTSWANA
Okavango Delta, the Jewel of Africa — 116

KENYA
Masai Mara Safari — 122

Asia — 128

INDIA
Palaces and Forts of Rajasthan — 130

MONGOLIA
Nomads of Khentii — 136

Australia & New Zealand — 142

AUSTRALIA
Snowy Mountains High Country — 144

NEW ZEALAND
Hurunui Backcountry Adventure — 150

Further Reading & Information — 156
Index — 158
Acknowledgements & Photo Credits — 157

Introduction

'You and your horse. His strength and beauty. Your knowledge and patience and determination. And understanding. And love. That's what fuses the two of you into this marvellous partnership that makes you wonder, what can Heaven offer any better than what you have here on earth?'

MONICA DICKENS

THIS BOOK IS THE RESULT OF A DEPRIVED CHILDHOOD, an unfulfilled dream and the marriage of two lifelong passions. It is dedicated to all the children who long to own a pony but, for whatever reason, never achieve that goal. It is also for those who never lost that fantasy of galloping off into the sunset on a winged steed, a fearless adventurer astride a gallant Pegasus.

My parents, of course, are to blame. Their stubborn refusal to give into my constant pleas for a horse only fed my obsession, driving me to exploit every opportunity I had to be near the creature of my desires. I was completely infatuated, and it was something my parents thought, and hoped, I would outgrow.

Something did happen, however, that would temper my obsession and put my dreams into perspective. When I turned 20, I discovered a new passion – travel – and like most young Australians, I took off on a yearlong trip around the world. It was then I accepted that horses, temporarily at least, would have to wait until I was in the financial and social situation to own one.

Twenty years later, I am still without a horse and leading a largely nomadic existence. Even family commitments have not kept me in one place for more than a few months at a time. The world keeps beckoning, and I keep following.

About ten years or so, however, I made a discovery that should have been obvious from the start – horses and travelling don't have to be mutually exclusive. I had always tried to incorporate a day's horse riding into my itineraries, but it hadn't actually dawned on me that horses could be the complete inspiration and focus for my travels, a means of transport as well as a partner in exploration.

It was while working as a researcher for a travel television program that I met a woman who would change and enrich my life – Nelly Gelich, the owner of Equitrek, an equine travel agency based in Sydney. She represents horse treks both in Australia and around the world. It was through Nelly that I realized this was the ultimate way of travelling for a horse lover like myself.

After my first multi-day trek in the Snowy Mountains' region of Australia I was hooked. Not only had I experienced sublime riding on wonderful horses, but also, for the first time, I understood what it was to be Australian, to be part of a landscape, culture and mythology. From the saddle, I saw sights impossible to experience any other way – intimate moments with wildlife, sweeping views from ridges and peaks far from vehicle access, and the quiet dignity of the Australian bush.

TOP LEFT *Horses take intrepid adventurers into some of the most remote corners of the world, places of mystery and beauty.*

LEFT *Horse and rider show equal interest as they examine spoor of wild animals in the Waterberg region of South Africa.*

All my other travel experiences, including five-star luxury holidays, pale in comparison to the simple pleasure of riding through the bush and camping under the southern sky. I realized that this was the only way to travel, and the one thing that made me feel completely happy.

I have since taken every opportunity to ride in other destinations around the world, joining long horse treks whenever possible. I have subsequently discovered many beautiful places, had incredible experiences and met wonderful people who also enjoy nature, love animals and have a spirit of adventure. Best of all, I have rekindled my relationship with the horse, rediscovered that neglected childhood passion and improved my riding ability tenfold!

Horseback travel is something that cannot be rushed. A wise horsewoman once told me, that you can only ride as fast as your horse can move! Like all vacations, the treks featured in this book require forward planning. Many of them are seasonal; some may not run annually because of political or economic crises. It would take a lifetime to actually see the whole world from the saddle, and I have only just begun my quest.

I must confess that I have not yet experienced all of the rides in this book, but those which I have not 'road tested' have been recommended by reputable agents who vouch for the high standards of service and horsemanship. I have also sought the advice of clients who have given me their unbiased opinions of each trek.

In the destinations featured, you will often find more than one riding organization offering horse treks, some of which are not mentioned in the copy. My apologies to those I have not disclosed, but please note that this book is by no means a listing of services. My intention is to evoke an experience, not to promote individuals or their operations.

Having said that, some of the best treks owe their success to individuals, and their efforts deserve recognition. I am also indebted to those who invited me to ride with them and share in

their unique lifestyles. Without their support, commitment and generosity, this book would not have been possible.

Then, of course, there are the quiet achievers – those magnificent, loyal and sometimes challenging horses that have made each ride memorable. I am amazed by the bond I form with my equine companions. I guess that's because riding is such a matter of faith. Every time I mount up, I am placing my trust in the horse – that he knows his job, is fit and capable of lasting the distance, and will stay on his feet. In an unfamiliar environment, you soon learn to appreciate that the horse

ABOVE *Magnificent scenery, companionship and an intimate relationship with four-legged friends – the hallmarks of a great riding holiday.*

knows the terrain better than you and wants to get himself home safely without mishap.

Of course, this does not always happen. It is important to remember that we are dealing with unpredictable creatures that do get scared, can act irrationally or simply make mistakes. On an unforgettable occasion, one of my mounts bucked hysterically, believing the loose cinch strap flapping around her feet was a very persistent snake. I was fortunate enough to anticipate her reaction, bailing out on the first buck and landing on my feet. I certainly could not blame the horse for being afraid.

Rider error is often the cause of accidents, but some situations are unavoidable. There is an old adage that a rider has to fall at least 100 times before he can be considered a true horseman. I'm not sure if I want to achieve that grand

figure, but I have had my share of spills, even off the horse I ride regularly.

Experience, of course, helps. The more I ride, the more secure my seat becomes and the more likely I am to stay put when my horse makes an unanticipated move. For this reason, I strongly recommend riding lessons prior to a horse-riding vacation, not only to learn the basics, but also to harden your body to the physical stress it will endure during a long trek. Six hours in the saddle is truly punishing if your muscles are soft and your body unaccustomed to such intense activity. Being saddle sore is not fun, but it can be avoided through care and preparation.

Even experienced riders, however, feel the effects of a long day's riding. Very few of us ride for six consecutive hours in our daily routine, so aching knees and thighs are a hazard that simply must be endured. After riding through amazing countryside on willing horses, however, it is sweet pain indeed, and it is amazing how those aches diminish after three days in the saddle.

Common sense is also imperative in avoiding saddle soreness. Smart riders wear comfortable clothing – closed-toed boots with a sensible heel, close-fitting jodhpurs, and long-sleeved shirts to reduce sunburn. Jeans are an easy, accessible and cheap alternative to riding breeches, but can cause painful grazes on the knee if the seams rub. Some people, even cowboys, recommend wearing nylon pantihose (tights) underneath

ABOVE *Wide open spaces and a rural ambience are features of riding in New Zealand, one of the most horse-friendly nations in the world.*

denim jeans to prevent chafing. Leather chaps are also a good, though expensive, alternative.

Like any adventure tour, a horse-riding holiday does have inherent risks. Riding is a dangerous sport, and there are countless cases of serious injuries and even deaths resulting from horse-related accidents. It is important that anyone considering a horse-riding tour appreciates the dangers and prepares for any circumstance.

For this reason, I never ride without a helmet, even when it is hot and uncomfortable doing so.

In Australia and some European countries, helmets are now mandatory by law, and it is likely that other destinations will follow suit as the liability issue rears its ugly head. Even in countries without legal requirements, many riding organizations insist that their clients wear helmets, both for peace of mind and insurance

reasons. Ironically, my most genuine cowboy ex-perience took place at a ranch where everyone, even the guides, wore helmets. Once the fashion element was eliminated, we could all get on with the job of driving cattle in relative safety.

Even on rides where helmets are optional, I strongly advise wearing one. Remember you will be riding an unfamiliar animal in new and often dangerous territory.

The issue of public liability is a complex one, and one I cannot fully explain in these pages. As the Western world becomes more obsessed with litigation, it will inevitably become a key issue in the equestrian world, and may well have a nega-tive impact on riding activities. I suggest taking out personal insurance before embarking on a riding holiday, checking the fine print to ensure that you are covered for dangerous sports.

One way of avoiding any grey legal areas is to book your riding adventures via a leading equine travel agency. It is their job to know if the oper-ator is fully insured, an issue that may be of par-ticular concern in Third World countries. The agency should also be able to advise you on per-sonal coverage, as well as assist in travel arrange-ments to and from the destination.

It is also reassuring to know that every ride represented by the agency has been assessed for its reliability, standard of horsemanship and the treatment of their animals. Sadly, there are many corrupt riding establishments in existence.

ABOVE *History, culture and a fine equestrian tra-dition combine on a ride in Rajasthan, India, home of the magnificent Marwari Horse.*

An agency can provide information and peace of mind, two things that are invaluable when planning a holiday.

What an agency cannot do, however, is guar-antee a brilliant holiday experience. You may run into bad weather, injure yourself or become ill. What they can and will do is point you in the right direction, help you find a ride that will best fulfil your needs. The actual experience of riding, absorbing and learning is then entirely up to you.

With its spectacular photography and descrip-tions of the world's most beautiful locations, *Great Horse Treks of the World* is designed to inspire you to mount up, gather the reins and move off into a world of horseback discovery. This is my book of dreams – thank you for shar-ing it with me.

Canadian Rockies Grandeur ☯ Bitterroot Roundup ☯ Cavalcade de Bravo

Rainforests of Costa Rica ☯ Torres Del Paine Vistas

Canadian Rockies Grandeur

Canadian Rockies Grandeur
ALBERTA, CANADA

Location *Banff National Park*

Getting there *Two-hour car or bus transfer from Calgary to Banff*

Season *April–October*

Duration *3–6 days tent and lodge trips; there are shorter rides available*

Group size *Maximum of 16 riders*

Horses *Mixed-breed geldings*

Tack *Western*

Pace *Slow*

Riding ability *All standards*

IT'S HARD TO IMAGINE ANYWHERE MORE PICTURE-perfect than Lake Louise – an exquisite, turquoise jewel in the Canadian Rockies. Circled by towering snowcapped peaks and flanked by forests of virgin pine, this beautiful mountain lake deserves its reputation as one of the world's top destinations, visited daily by throngs of admiring tourists anxious to capture its remarkable beauty.

Forty kilometres (25 miles) south, it's a very different scenario at an equally idyllic location. A small group of trail riders has paused for lunch on the deserted shores of Rainbow Lake, deep in Banff National Park. A campfire crackles, coffee on the boil; and a lone fisherman tries his luck, casting onto the lake's mirrored surface. Suddenly, a hush descends on the group as a grizzly bear appears in the distance, frolicking on a glacier with her playful cub. It is the perfect wilderness moment, an unforgettable encounter indelibly etched on every mind.

Such are the joys of exploring Canada's mountain trails on horseback. In the saddle, modern-day adventurers can go beyond the popular tourist traps, delving into an untouched wilderness where harmony, tranquillity and a pioneering spirit endure. Breathtaking vistas abound at every corner, with sun-kissed glacial peaks piercing a cloudless blue sky, alpine meadows strewn with wildflowers, bubbling mountain streams and azure lakes, peaceful havens of rest for riders and their mounts.

On winding trails, four sturdy legs pick their way over ruts and rocks, ever deeper into the forest. Wildlife abounds – elk, deer, the occasional bear, and eagles soaring on mountain thermals. Human presence is minimal, with only the odd bush walker to share the solitude. Here in the remote backcountry, the only access is on foot, whether two or four – even park rangers pack supplies on horses and mules, with the rocky terrain impractical for motorized vehicles.

Horseback exploration of the Canadian Rockies is a tradition dating back to pioneer days, when railway workers and adventurers forged routes through the Western wilderness. The remote valleys and passes were already well known to the native tribes of the Rockies; local indigenous guides often assisted early European explorers in their quest. Exploration of the Bow Valley surrounding Calgary began in 1800. Fifty years later, the Palliser Expedition focused attention on the remarkable beauty of the Banff mountains. In 1883, three railroad workers stumbled across a series of hot springs beneath what is now called Sulphur Mountain; and after a heated ownership dispute, the springs and surrounding area were set aside as Canada's first national park.

Today, Banff National Park is a 6641km^2 (2564sq.miles) recreational park offering over 1500km (932 miles) of backcountry trails, 53 campgrounds, and thousands of acres of world-class ski terrain. Eight million awestruck visitors annually cannot be wrong – this indeed is one of the world's great beauty spots, unspoiled, pristine, a place which remains as nature intended.

PREVIOUS PAGES *A wrangler saddles horses in the corral at Bitterroot Ranch, Wyoming.*
ABOVE LEFT *Strong, surefooted and reliable mules are still utilized on the challenging trails of the Canadian Rockies, harking back to pioneer days.*
OPPOSITE *Horse riders must be prepared to cross many rivers on the four-day riding trail in the Banff National Park.*

Fortunately for horse lovers, riding the trails of Banff National Park is actively encouraged, with only a few of the more environmentally delicate trails closed to four-legged traffic. Riders simply need to obtain a wilderness pass and a grazing permit to take their own horses into the park overnight; they are then left to their own devices and common sense to minimize impact and enjoy the tranquillity.

The riding season in the Canadian Rockies is brief, with the weather dictating its boundaries. Typically, the trails are accessible from May to October, although spring floods or unseasonable snowfalls can be hazardous. Midsummer is typically sunny and warm; however, mountain weather can be moody and unpredictable. Chilly nights often reach subzero temperatures, making warm clothing and top-quality sleeping bags absolute necessities.

For those who don't own a horse, or overseas visitors keen to explore the park further, there are a couple of commercial operators that offer guided trips of varying duration. The largest of these is Warner Guiding and Outfitting in Banff, a slick and professional operation with 41 years of experience and over 300 horses.

ABOVE *A wrangler leads his pack mule, and a group of riders across Healy Creek on the way to Sundance Lodge.*

OPPOSITE *Riders on the shore of spectacular Rainbow Lake, one of the most picturesque lunch sites imaginable!*

With Banff's city shopfront and three working stables, this company does a roaring trade attracting everyone from busloads of Japanese tourists to genuine horse enthusiasts looking for new equine adventures.

Beginners are usually satisfied with one of the short morning trail rides along the base of Sulphur Mountain, or a Covered Wagon Cookout offering a taste of the Canadian Wild West. More experienced riders, however, have the option of joining pack trips ranging from two to six days with a choice of staying in either comfortable backcountry lodges or Warner's exclusive camp grounds.

The lodge trips are of great appeal to those who prefer their creature comforts. Overnight accommodation is in delightful log cabins that are fully equipped with hot and cold running water, country kitchens, as well as warm beds to curl up in after a long day's ride. These genuine backcountry refuges, with a wealth of local history, have welcomed weary travellers for over 70 years.

Riders on the tenting trips in the Cascade Valley have access to simpler luxuries such as washstands with hot water, large A-frame tents, rustic outhouses, and a fire pit for evening socializing and a mandatory campfire sing-along. A large kitchen tent warmed by a welcoming

day, much of that at an altitude of around 2100m (6890ft) above sea level. The ascents can be heart stopping and the descents downright dangerous. River crossings and rocky trails put undue stress on tendons and hooves; gopher holes are another hazard. It is testament to the reliability and sturdiness of the trail horses that they make the distance in one piece.

Warner's trail horses are certainly placid animals, content to follow head-to-tail along the single-file track. Only geldings are used – mares are temperamental beasts and have been known to attract unwanted attention from wild game. While they may not be the most handsome or purebred horses in the world, Warner's string are generally fit, strong and reliable, with calm, unflappable natures – the perfect trail companions. All are trained to neck rein and are ridden in long-stirrup Western saddles.

Accompanying each ride is a pack mule carting lunch and picnic supplies, while luggage and sleeping bags are transported from camp to camp by a further string of eight or nine mules – a unique feature of Canadian rides, and a fascinating link to pioneering days. Guests love to

wood fire provides the setting for ranch-style meals prepared by talented young cooks who appear to relish their isolated lifestyle.

Three camps, each with its own character and charm, are utilized on this trail. Stoney Camp sits on the banks of a river bubbling beneath the magnificent Palliser Range; Flints Park Camp is nestled in the shadow of eerie Flints Peak; while at Mystic Camp, which lies on the 40 Mile Pass, stands of old pine and spruce trees creating a mystical ambience.

With the long summer twilight, the hours at camp are casual and relaxed, with fishing expeditions and roping competitions fuelling the growing camaraderie between guests and wranglers. Two local cowboys, with a genuine interest in the environment and a passion for the Western lifestyle, accompany each ride. Canadian cowboys like to think of themselves

as the real deal – they talk the talk, walk the walk and they don them in outfits straight from a John Wayne movie. Ten-gallon hats, spurred boots, checked shirts and fringed 'chinks' (three-quarter length chaps) are all part of the ideal, along with a mean lasso twirl. It's an image beloved by the tourists; in fact, many guests join the costume party, becoming self-styled Marlboro men and women for the duration of their trip.

For all the cowboy bravado, however, Banff rides are relatively tame, the pace dictated by rugged terrain and the presence of the pack mules. The ride is conducted almost exclusively at a walk making it the perfect adventure for less experienced riders or even youngsters.

Despite the lack of speed, the rides can be gruelling for horse and rider. Fifteen to twenty-five kilometres (9–15 miles) are covered each

ABOVE *Close encounters with wildlife – such as this magnificent bull elk – is a highlight of a ride through the Canadian Rockies.*

RIGHT *One of Warner's pack mules waits patiently for the load of lunch and picnic supplies to be unhitched from its back.*

watch the time-consuming process of packing; it's important that the loads are evenly balanced to avoid injury to the mule's back. Once the packs are in place, they are then secured with the famous 'diamond hitch'.

For long-distance packing, mules appear to be the equine of choice. They can easily carry up to 90kg (198 pounds), are cheaper to feed, more surefooted and won't spook as easily as horses. Besides, they don't have the attitude problem that some pack horses develop!

As horses and mules pick their way contentedly along the narrow trails, riders find themselves with plenty of time to contemplate the magnificent scenery surrounding them. Dense forests of Douglas Fir, lodge-pole pines and spruce open to high, rocky ridges offering 180-degree views of snowcapped mountain peaks and imposing cliff faces soaring above the tree line, are but a few of the awe-inspiring features offered by this region. Occasionally you'll come across an avalanche site, massive boulders strewn haphazardly by nature's fury. River crossings provide a welcome break and photo opportunity as your horse pauses to drink the cool, glacial liquid. High meadows are another enticement, a luscious feeding ground of rich grasses and wildflowers; while an historic elk corral is a reminder of a not-so-distant pioneering past. Then there is every nature-lover's favourite pastime – wildlife

BELOW *A cowboy, decked out in authentic chinks and a ten-gallon hat, takes a quick nap against the rails of an historic elk corral.*

spotting. Every trip provides a new, exciting story to write home about – a coyote dashing across the path; the flash of an elusive cougar; a doe, head raised in alarm; or a grizzly bear stalking beyond the electric fence surrounding the camp ground.

For adventurers with a genuine interest in wildlife research, Warner Guiding and Outfitting also runs a series of wildlife monitoring expeditions which operates in conjunction with Parks Canada. These trips offer riders the once-in-a-lifetime opportunity to assist with valuable wildlife research, helping to document the behaviour and habits of grizzly bears and wolves. It's a fantastic opportunity to spend time in one of Canada's richest wildlife corridors and to help protect these wonderful animals for future generations to appreciate.

Bitterroot Roundup

Bitterroot Roundup
WYOMING, USA

Location *Bitterroot Ranch, Dubois*

Getting there *Transfer by car or taxi from*
 Jackson Hole

Season *June–October*

Duration *8 days*

Group size *Maximum of 16 riders*

Horses *Arab; local ranch-bred horses*

Tack *Western; helmets compulsory*

Pace *Moderate to fast*

Riding ability *Novice to advanced*

INSIDE EVERY HORSE-LOVING MAN AND WOMAN lurks the heart of a cowboy. Whether we ride English style or Western, childhood fantasies of roping and riding are etched into our souls, drawing us into dreams of wide open plains, of happy trails, and a campfire sing-along under a starlit sky. A cowboy represents adventure, heroism and freedom – the embodiment of a pioneering spirit with simple values and a carefree existence. He is our inspiration and role model, galloping off into the sunset on his trusty steed.

This romantic ideal is at the core of the 'dude ranch' culture in the United States of America. Capitalizing on the timeless appeal of Hollywood Westerns, many working cattle ranches have opened their doors to paying guests, inviting them to share in their daily routine and experience a taste of Wild West hospitality.

There are literally hundreds of these establishments to choose from, all catering to different clientele requirements. Some, for instance, have a kitschy 'theme park' quality about them, offering a pseudo-Western experience with chuckwagon rides, staged Indian attacks, square dances and cookouts. Others offer a more genuine working environment where guests learn new skills and develop their riding ability as they pitch in with seasonal cattle duties.

Some ranches offer resort facilities and an endless array of organized activities; others accommodate guests in simple, rustic cabins in keeping with old West traditions. Whatever your holiday requirements, the motivation is universal – the realization of dreams, fulfilment of fantasies and the search for new inspiration. A midlife crisis, for instance, was the catalyst for Billy Crystal's Western adventure in the classic Hollywood comedy, *City Slickers*. 'Go and find your smile,' his tolerant wife advised before he headed off on Curly's cattle drive.

Billy found his smile, and so have many others who followed enthusiastically in his footsteps, inspired to have a similar, life-changing experience in the saddle.

It is to the glorious Rocky Mountain states of Montana, Wyoming and Colorado where most people head for their cowboy experience. Blessed with soaring peaks, breathtaking vistas and millions of hectares (acres) of wilderness, these regions offer limitless riding opportunities in a vast frontier landscape.

Even in God's own country, however, ranch experiences may vary. In some places you can ride all day in absolute solitude, while others are located on a main drag where riding trails are compromised by encroaching suburbia. Some ranches have access to high mountains but rocky, difficult paths may restrict riding opportunities. It is certainly worth researching what sort of ground you will be covering during your stay, as it may dictate the pace of riding and your subsequent level of enjoyment.

However, few ranches allow their guests to gallop around at will, regardless of terrain. Liability issues have resulted in many rides being conducted exclusively at a walk. Serious riders should ask about the pace and frequency of outings, the size of each riding group, and

ABOVE LEFT *A newborn Arabian foal learns an early appreciation of the magnificent summer wildflowers at Bitterroot Ranch in Wyoming.*

OPPOSITE *A group of trail riders pauses during a trek through the pine and aspen landscape of the Shoshone National Forest.*

whether guests are evaluated on their level of horsemanship before setting off on the trail. A little research should reveal the sort of establishment you are dealing with.

Another point to consider is whether the ranch owns its horses, or simply rents them for the season. While this may be the cheapest option during a brief vacation period, ranches that lease their horses have little control over the quality or education of their animals. A ranch that breeds and trains its own horses is more likely to offer a safe and supervised riding environment where the welfare of the animals is as important as that of the riders.

On some American ranches, increased safety concerns and insurance demands have resulted in the demise of a beloved Western icon – the cowboy hat. On Wyoming's Bitterroot Ranch, for instance, all riders, including wranglers, must wear helmets on the trail. 'What matters is the safety of my guests and my staff,' says ranch owner Bayard Fox, who, despite 65 years of riding, also dons a regulation black crash helmet. 'If that makes me unpopular, that's just bad luck.'

Despite fashion being off the agenda, Bitterroot Ranch still manages to capture true Western spirit and adventure in its challenging

yet exciting riding programme. Here, the cowboy experience comes naturally – there are no contrived scenarios, no campfires, and no artificial drawls. What you have instead is the simple formula of good horses, fun-loving company, hard work and awe-inspiring Wyoming scenery – the stuff that legends are truly made of.

For those unfamiliar with the territory, the state of Wyoming is an intriguing panorama; its ever-changing moods a constant and delightful surprise. Baking desert badlands, carved into eerie moonscapes by nature's deft chisel give way to dusty fields of fragrant sage and flowering prickly pear, the perfect location for a headlong gallop. Rocky outcrops, resonant with the ghosts of outlaws, lead to death-defying gorges slashed by mountain streams raging with glacial runoff. As the altitude changes the scenery softens to the aroma of pine and aspen, dense forests opening to woodland meadows dotted with lupine, phlox and the exquisite red blooms of the Indian paintbrush. Winding trails emerge onto lofty ridges, offering expansive views of the snowcapped peaks of the Continental Divide, a sparkling tiara against an endless blue horizon.

Bitterroot, nestled in this chameleonic location, is the last ranch in a remote valley bordering the Shoshone National Forest, with 80km (50 miles) of unspoiled wilderness separating it from the Yellowstone Park. The closest reminder of civilization is 40 minutes away at Dubois, an historic outpost with the typical appearance of a Hollywood film set – wooden boardwalks, log buildings, 'good-ol'-boy' saloon and quite a number of pick-up trucks. This was once the stomping ground of Butch Cassidy and his notorious gang who hid out in the nearby badlands during their bandit reign.

Part of the Greater Yellowstone Ecosystem, the Shoshone National Forest consists of 971,280ha (2,400,000 acres) of some of the wildest countryside remaining in the lower 48 states – a rich habitat for elk, bighorn sheep, mountain goats and grizzly bears. It is also home to Bitterroot's cattle during the summer months, providing lush grazing pastures in over 130km^2 (50sq. miles) of high mountains, heavily timbered forests and the valleys of the Wind River.

LEFT *Bitterroot Ranch caters to all standards of riders, but those with previous riding experience appreciate the variety of terrain and the excellent standard of horses on offer.*

An important part of the Bitterroot calendar is the annual cattle drive where guests, who ride well enough, participate in the routine of a working cowboy, driving the cows deep into the forest. This is time-consuming and unpredictable work requiring long hours in the saddle at elevations of up to 3048m (10,000ft), which is a physically demanding experience for horse and rider. For first-time cowboys, applying new skills learned on the job is an intense and fun challenge, one that requires independence and teamwork with fellow wranglers.

ABOVE *Rocky bluffs fuel thoughts of outlaws and noon shootouts in the Wild West.*
RIGHT *Guests take on genuine cowboy duties during the annual cattle drive, herding breeding stock to higher elevations.*

The most rewarding partnership, however, is that of horse and rider as they attempt to predict the movement of the herd. Many of Bitterroot's Arabs are excellent cow ponies and know their job well. These horses drive the cows and calves in the right direction with a feisty attitude, quick thinking and the occasional nip on the nearest bovine bum. As a wise old cowboy once said, 'When in doubt, let your horse do the thinking'.

ABOVE *Ranch owner Bayard Fox and his dear old friend Traveler – an indomitable partnership with a combined age of over 100 years!*
OPPOSITE *Bitterroot's herd of beautifully bred Arabs is brought into the corral on an early morning roundup.*

Bitterroot's string of 180 Arab and Quarter horses are most certainly an impressive herd; handsome, beautifully bred and well educated by Bayard's wife Mel. In the corral, Kenyan-born Mel rules with an iron fist in a velvet glove, demanding high levels of discipline and horsemanship from staff and guests alike. For some horse riders this is their foray into Western riding, and old-school English habits must be discarded as they learn to control their mounts on a loose rein with minimal interference.

Complementing Mel's strict, eagle-eyed instruction, Bayard Fox charms and delights with his devil-may-care attitude to life on the ranch. Seventy-six years old, this fit and wiry rancher is a passionate and entertaining guide as he shares his knowledge of his custodial land and its fascinating history. With a cheeky glint in his eye, he zealously speaks of pioneering days, of Butch and Sundance, long winters and numerous encounters with wildlife. 'If you've been to Wyoming, you've seen the world,' he tells his guests proudly.

Age has certainly not wearied this accomplished horseman, who has ridden in over 30 countries. After apologizing for the combined age of himself and his 28-year-old horse Traveler – over 100 years – Bayard surprised us all by wheeling his trusty steed around and giving him free rein, bounding up a hill and across the sagebrush plain like a streak of white lightning.

As my little Arab mare strained to keep up with this furious pace, dust flying from under pounding hooves and wind whipping through her mane, I began to appreciate Mel's philosophy of absolute trust in my horse. Surefooted on the undulating hillsides and comfortable on the scrubby trail, our mounts were powerhouses of equine energy galloping with unrestrained joy. Holding them back was never an option; they would stop when they had had enough.

This is the cowboy experience at its purest – riding willing horses in wide open spaces, unfettered by fences, roads and artificial barriers. By letting go and opening one's mind to new experiences, a new level of freedom is reached which helps you find a new perspective on life. It certainly helped me find my smile!

Cavalcade de Bravo

Cavalcade de Bravo
VALLE DE BRAVO, MEXICO

Location *Finca Enyhe, Valle de Bravo*

Getting there *A 2-hour car transfer from Mexico City*

Season *November–March*

Duration *7 days*

Group size *2–8 riders*

Horses *Criollo; Trakehner, Quarter Horse*

Tack *English, Western or Mexican* charro

Pace *Moderate*

Riding ability *Intermediate to advanced*

HORSE RIDING IS OFTEN PERCEIVED AS A GLAMOROUS pastime, an elitist activity for a privileged few. Those who have ever heaved a leaden saddle onto a horse's back know better – the reality of riding is more about blood, sweat, broken bones and dirty fingernails than champagne and canapés. Sore muscles, days without showers and sleepless nights on rock-hard ground are common features of horse trekking, and those with a true sense of adventure and a love of the outdoors wouldn't have it any other way.

Every now and then, however, one longs for a soft, downy bed, gourmet meal, and an indulgent massage in an exotic location. In our dreams we are in a Mexican hacienda, swaying in a hammock, margarita in hand, evocative strains of mariachi music wafting on a balmy breeze. But this fantasy includes horses; their glorious canters across soft grasslands, hooves beating on fallen pine needles and endless mountain views from a carved saddle bedecked with silver.

This, of course, is a Mexico worlds away from tawdry border towns and shoddy coastal resorts. It also belies the image of the lonely *vaquero* riding through dusty, wild desert littered with cacti and rattlesnakes, a scenario beloved by Hollywood film makers.

Mexico, the struggling and overcrowded nation south of the US border, is a land of extremes – and horse-riding opportunities are no different. For pure adventure in one of the harshest, most challenging terrains, a pack excursion into remote Copper Canyon will fulfil every Wild West fantasy, rampaging *banditos* and all! This is as wild as the West can possibly get; in fact, this trip has been compared to travelling in the Rockies during the 1880s. Riders must be prepared for long hours in the saddle, inhospitable terrain, dangerous inclines, unpredictable schedules and primitive facilities along the trail – a challenge for even the most hardened horse trekker.

On the other extreme is the ride called La Sierra Cavalcade, which combines a five-star vacation experience with excellent riding in a beautiful location. Forget about hard work, simple meals and roughing it – on this ride, the only finger you'll lift is the one on the reins as you wheel in your mount after an invigorating canter.

The base for this romantically dubbed cavalcade is Valle de Bravo, a picturesque 400-year-old town located two-and-a-half-hours west of Mexico City, in the heart of the Sierra Madre Occidental mountain range. With its quaint cobblestone streets, white stucco buildings and colourful handicraft markets, this prosperous little town is a popular weekend retreat for city families who come to breathe the clean mountain air. The temperate climate is ideal for hikes in the evergreen forests or to relax in the delightful lakeside setting.

Among the town's imposing colonial structures is Finca Enyhe, a guesthouse owned and operated by endurance rider José Schravesande (also known as Pepe) and his wife, Lucia. With its large stable, excellent riding arena and top-quality horses, Finca Enyhe is considered one

ABOVE LEFT *Cavalcade hostess, Lucia, with one of her beautiful riding horses, bedecked in a typical Mexican* charro *saddle and bridle.*

OPPOSITE *The hosts dress in traditional Mexican riding gear, an indication of the finery and class of this exceptional riding holiday.*

of the highest-calibre riding centres in Central America, attracting horse enthusiasts from all over the world.

From the moment visitors arrive at the guesthouse, they know they are in for a special experience. A bamboo-lined driveway leads past manicured gardens ablaze with the tropical hues of palms, bougainvillea and bird-of-paradise flowers. The restored hacienda, an imposing five-metre (15ft) façade decorated with wrought iron, is built around a large central courtyard, with a fountain bubbling peacefully and hammocks swaying from under stucco archways. The setting is elegant and a reminder of genteel days from a colonial past.

After being greeted by their hosts, guests are shown to their rooms, which are airy and spacious with private bathrooms, all embellished with an eclectic collection of antique and regional Mexican furniture. Thereafter, lunch is served under a pergola, heavily laden with purple wisteria; a tranquil setting for an authentic

---

ABOVE *The vibrant colours of Mexico are reflected in Mother Nature's artistry on one of the mountain trails high above Valle de Bravo.*

Guests are encouraged to immerse themselves in Mexican culture – indulge in a siesta, explore the village, buy handicrafts from local artisans, and gorge on Lucia's delicious culinary inventions, washed down by tequila and margaritas.

Pepe and Lucia are gracious hosts – who both speak flawless English and are well informed about local history, culture, wildlife and the special geographic features of the area. They are also excellent riders, a crucial prerequisite on any world-standard horse trek, and lead the cavalcade themselves.

Mexico has a rich equestrian tradition dating back to the Spanish conquistadors, who first introduced the natives to horses and cattle. The clash of these two cultures – subservience followed by violence and rebellion – led to the creation of the *charro*, Mexico's famous cowboy. With their wide-brimmed sombreros and handlebar-shaped moustaches, *charros* figure prominently in Mexico's national anthem and ride proudly in the annual Independence Day parades.

In keeping with the *charro* tradition, horses hold pride of place at Finca Enyhe. The wooden-beamed tack room is a treasure-trove of leather, silver and embroidery on tack ranging from English-style Stubbens to heavily carved and decorated Mexican saddles. These impressive works of art are characterized by a wide seat and a large pommel; some also have a decorative machete attached to one side.

Pepe's horses are handsome and exceptionally well bred, a far cry from the scruffy little pack animals usually associated with rural Mexico. His string includes Trakehners, Thoroughbreds, Quarter Horses and Appendix (Quarter/Thoroughbred cross) as well as tough little Criollos, descended from horses brought to the Americas by the Spanish. Most of the horses are well over

Mexican feast. The meal offers a selection of regional specialties, fresh home-grown produce and Spanish wine. And so the scene is set for a week of indulgence and comfort.

RIGHT *Mexican, English and Spanish saddles – some adorned with silver, others embroidered – are stored in the tack room at Finca Enyhe.*

16 hands, well trained and fit enough to cope with vigorous ascents in the high altitude. Horses are matched to the ability of the riders before embarking on the trail.

Every day riders set out from Finca Enyhe, and return each afternoon by car while the horses stay in the woods, attended by diligent grooms who ride with the group. Also accompanying each ride is the hardy pack mule Don Sabino, responsible for carting the ingredients for an alfresco lunch served in a spectacular location – the grooms also assist with lunch preparation.

The route explored on the circular cavalcade is a pastoral scene, a colourful kaleidoscope of rural Mexican life. Stately haciendas flank simple peasant allotments; burros loaded with firewood trot through narrow cobbled lanes, while open farmlands afford riders the opportunity for a fast canter. Each day has its highlights – a spectacular view of the valley from the peak of Monte Alto; a narrow trail leading into El Hoyo, a collapsed volcanic crater; an eerie black lagoon; or the viewpoint from a majestic rocky knoll known as Los Tres Reyes – 'the three kings'.

An ever-present feature on the cavalcade is the man-made lake of Valle de Bravo, which supplies water to the surrounding villages. Viewed from the mountain peaks it is a shimmering mirage, and along its marshy shore it provides the opportunity for a wet and wild gallop. At the end of one of the day rides, guests are transported back to the Finca by boat, gliding silently across the azure waters of the lake – a meditative conclusion to a long day in the saddle.

Valle de Bravo is located at 1829m (6000ft) above sea level, and riders climb to the lofty heights of the Sierra Madre mountain range, which is around 3657m (12,000ft), where they are exposed to a wide variety of plant and animal life, and experience several different microclimates. Fruit trees – avocado, orange, plum, peach, Mexican guava, *chirimoya*, *guanabana* and *zapote* – as well as a variety of flowers line the lower pathways. The trail climbs into cool, silent forests of endemic oak and over 100 species of pine trees, providing habitat for more than 300 species

ABOVE *Riders cool their horses – hot and dusty after a long day crossing mountainous terrain – in the lake of Valle de Bravo.*

of birds including the golden eagle, endangered thick-billed parrot and the tufted jay.

At about 3000m (10,000ft), the horses are tied to trees and the riders climb the rest of the way on foot to a little-known and rarely visited sanctuary. During the months of November to March, each excursion includes a visit to the Monarch Butterfly Sanctuary to witness an amazing natural phenomenon – millions of orange-winged butterflies that have descended on the warm forests of Mexico's central highlands. Here, in the shade of the forest, the butterflies that migrate every year from colder northern climes cling to the pine boughs, making the trees appear to be dead oaks. Suddenly, a ray of sunshine will strike and a delicate whirring begins as thousands of butterflies become air-

borne, fluttering, feeding, mating, blanketing the sky with shades of gold as they prepare for their long flight home to Canada.

'That moment when the sun streams into the forest and the butterflies begin flying is beyond description. One can even hear the sound of their wings... You don't dare talk or move. All five senses are focused on witnessing and enjoying the grandiose nature of what you are living,' Paloma Palomino recalled the experience.

To observe these butterflies is an incomparable experience; some claim it to be a spiritual

ABOVE *The superb colonial stables at Finca Enyhe encapsulate the Mexican experience of living history and vibrant traditions.*

awakening to hear the whirr of millions of fluttering wings reverberating through the still air. For all its luxury and first-class service, the highlight of the La Sierra Cavalcade trek comes free of charge, a beautiful gift courtesy of Mother Nature.

After a week of superlative riding, pampering, relaxation, and encounters with nature that leave you breathless with admiration, the final return to Finca Enyhe, this time on horseback, is always emotional. As the horses are unsaddled, the passionate strains of music waft into the stable, and a group of *charros* dressed in black appear, strumming their guitars, blowing trumpets and singing 'La Negra'. It's a fitting farewell after an amazing equestrian experience that offers the best of Mexico.

From Pacific Beach to Cloud Forest

From Pacific Beach to Cloud Forest

CENTRAL PACIFIC REGION, COSTA RICA

Location *Maravilla Ranch*

Getting there *Transfer from San José*

Season *December–August*

Duration *8–10 days*

Group size *2–8 riders*

Horse *Costa Rican Criollo; mixed breeds*

Tack *Local* tico

Pace *Moderate*

Riding ability *Intermediate to advanced*

WE TREAD LIGHTLY THROUGH THE VELVET JUNGLE, hoof beats muffled by the spongy moss underfoot. A shaft of sunlight pierces the mist, illuminating the path before us, exposing its verdant emerald underbelly, a dense carpet of ferns and orchids, bromeliads and lichen. In the dense silence there is a cacophony – the rustle of lizards through the undergrowth; the screech of a howler monkey swinging through the canopy; the courtship song of an elusive quetzal; the gentle exhalation of a horse's breath as it fills its lungs with the cool, pure air. This pocket of perfection is Costa Rica!

Nature's bounty is at its most abundant in Costa Rica. This tiny nation located near the equator between Nicaragua and Panama covers only 0.03 per cent of the earth's surface, yet it is endowed with over five per cent of all the life forms on earth. It is a fecund display of tropical biodiversity – there are over 13,000 plant species (including 1500 trees and 1400 types of orchid), more than 850 species of bird, 209 different mammals and 220 species of reptile. Also, the crawling creatures relish this environment, with over 350,000 species of arthropod identified here, and 10 per cent of the world's butterflies are found in this region.

Life flourishes in a diversity of habitats, from dry savanna to mysterious cloud forests. There are 11 volcanoes, various hot springs, two beautiful coastlines, pristine beaches, mountains, plains, valleys and forests. It has more protected area than any other country in the world, with more than 16 per cent of the countryside zoned as parks, wildlife refuges and forest reserves. These statistics help to explain why hundreds of thousands of ecologically minded tourists are lured to this natural wonderland each year. Twenty-five years ago, Costa Rica actually launched the Eco-tourism trend, inventing the concept of sustainable tourism to promote the care of the environment. In a region where nations continually struggle to reconcile man's impact on nature, Costa Rica is a model of conservational harmony.

Eco-tourism means responsible travel to natural areas, tourism that has low impact on the environment and local culture while generating an income for its people. In Costa Rica, it is an economic philosophy that appears to be working. Not only has the country avoided the political upheavals of its neighbours, but it also has a strong health-care system and a literacy rate of 98 per cent, one of the highest in the world. Mother Nature has been generous, and the *ticos* have reaped the rewards for responsible stewardship of the land.

There are many ways of exploring this tropical paradise without impacting on it. A walking tour accompanied by a naturalist guide will open your mind to the details of the rainforest. Canopy tours give travellers a chance to experience the upper levels of the forest where it bustles with activity; while a paddle in a sea kayak will show the wonders of Costa Rica's amazing coastline.

However, one of the most popular ways of getting around is on horseback. A number of spectacular tours offers a chance to explore the

ABOVE LEFT *The Irazú Volcano – its main crater filled with a pea-green coloured lake – is one of many attractions in Costa Rica.*

OPPOSITE *Horses are available for hire everywhere in Costa Rica, whether on the beach or through a professional organization.*

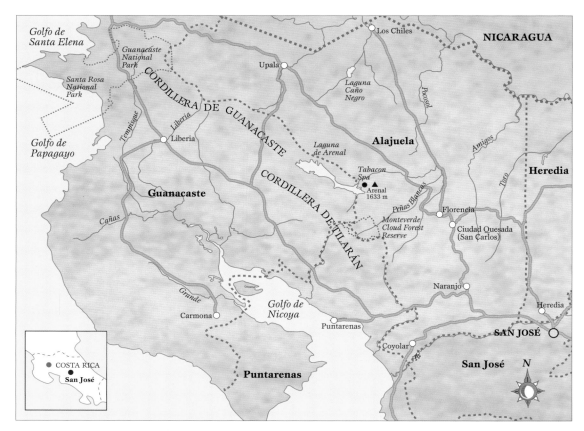

country's diversity of landscapes. Horses are something of a national pastime in Costa Rica, with its history indelibly linked to the life of the cowboy, or *sabanero* as the local *ticos* call them. What better way to show off their two great passions – horses and their land – than on an international riding holiday?

Some tour operators, such as Costa Rican Horse Adventures (previously known as Eco-Safari Adventures), have joined forces with local ranch owners who offer access to their land, stock and accommodation with the aim of promoting adventure horse treks that benefit the local community. Most of the horses are farm bred – placid and docile enough to be level-headed over rugged ground, but agile and nimble-footed during a dash down a long, sandy beach.

The original horses brought to the Americas by the Spanish were much smaller animals – they were a hardy breed that managed to survive generations of neglect, rough terrain and extremes of weather. In the past 35 years, imported bloodlines such as the magnificent Andalucians, Peruvian Pasos, Quarter Horses and Arabs have been introduced, complementing the sturdy Spanish horse to create a remarkably calm, sure-footed and handsome riding animal known as the Costa Rican Criollo.

True to the *sabanero* culture, these horses are ridden in a simple rope bozal, which is a bitless bridle that works like a hackamore. They have been taught to neck rein and also obey voice commands. The saddles are modified McClellan and Western saddles, with deep seats, high cantles and either closed or open stirrups. Those used to English riding may take a while to adjust to this more casual style, but they will soon find that their horses respond better over long distances when ridden on a loose rein.

With tourism being such an integral part of the Costa Rican economy, it's no surprise that the *ticos* are renowned for their warmth, hospitality and grace. Everyone is welcome in their paradise,

---

ABOVE LEFT *A gallop along one of Costa Rica's many pristine beaches is a popular feature of trekking in this eco-friendly country.*

even nervous beginner riders who may wish to combine their horse-riding adventure with other activities. Children are also catered for on the tours with a special package designed around the needs of travelling families.

The evocatively named Odyssey tour is Costa Rican Horse Adventures' premier ride – a treat for serious riders with a spirit of adventure and a thirst for exploration. This is a movable feast; a ride designed to showcase the best of Costa Rica, traversing the country's most scenic regions. Beautiful beaches, sweeping savanna, mountain ranges and forests – it's all here, Costa Rica encapsulated in a 10-day ride.

Three separate bases are utilized on this ride, each providing access to a unique habitat and landscape. Riders are given the maximum time and optimum opportunity to explore each region; they are then transferred by vehicle to the next base where the adventure continues.

One of Costa Rica's most idyllic riding areas is the Dry Central Pacific Region with its rolling hills, open meadows, and transitional forests teeming with wildlife. Home during this portion of the ride is the Hacienda La Maravilla, a working cattle ranch located near the Cuarros River

on the Pacific coast. Life at this pretty hacienda is friendly and informal; guests are encouraged to join in the daily routines of the farm and absorb the *sabanero* lifestyle on display.

Mother Nature's picnic basket literally drips off the trees in this lush, tropical haven. The fruit is ripe for the picking – sweet bananas hacked straight from the tree using a machete; juicy, mouthwatering mangoes; coconuts freshly split for its thirst-quenching milk. Every meal is a veritable feast – ingredients include chayote squash, sweet potatoes, cassava and avocado balancing the *ticos'* staple of rice and beans flavoured with mild tropical spices. And of course, accompanying every meal is the legendary Costa Rican coffee.

In many ways, Costa Rica is like a large tropical island. Only 177km (110 miles) separates the Atlantic from the Pacific at its narrowest point, and a beautiful beach is never more than

ABOVE *Lake Arenal covers an area of approximately 124km² (48 square miles), making it the largest lake in Costa Rica.*

LEFT *A* tico *rider shows off the simple local tack – Western style saddle with leather stirrups and a rope bozal bridle.*

TOP *The carnivorous red-eyed tree frog* (Agalychnis callisdryas) *is found in South America and most parts of Central America.*

ABOVE *The verdant trails on Costa Rica's mountainous interior reveal a number of microclimates, and a diversity of flora.*

121km (75 miles) away. The white sand and crystal clear waters are a magnet for appreciative tourists; none more so than horse riders who delight in the sensual pleasure of pounding along a deserted beach on a fiery steed.

'Let's pick up the pace,' José shouted. The horses seemed to understand. Estrella executed a courbette and shot down the stretch of sand. I suddenly realized how powerful and surefooted this incredible animal was. For a minute, my whole world centred on staying aboard as we accelerated. Adrenaline still pumping, I relaxed my shoulders and leaned into the gallop. Estrella's pace reflected my improved position and her gait became smoother and faster. I was astride Pegasus, flying along the deserted tropical beach, the wind in my face. My childhood dream had come true.

This is the coastline where the Spanish began their conquest of Central America back in 1561. History devotees will get a kick out of following their very trail, crossing the slip of land formerly known as the Port of Landecho before splashing through the Cascajalillo Mangrove Swamp en route to the blissful Bajamar Beach.

The pace of the Odyssey ride slows considerably as the group ascends, quite literally, into the clouds. Enveloped almost continuously by fog and mist, the Cloud Forests of Costa Rica are hotbeds of biodiversity, harbouring a plethora of plants and animals that are found nowhere else in the world. The array of lush green plants is staggering – trees are covered with mosses, bromeliads, ferns and at least 878 species of epiphyte. The overall effect is of a verdant garden suffocating under its own weight and strangled by choking roots and vines.

Straddling the Continental Divide, the Monteverde Cloud Forest begins at an elevation of 1350m (4430ft), peaking at the top of the Tilaran Mountains at 1850m (6070ft). Trees at the lower levels form a soaring forest canopy, while at the top constant winds and rain have stunted tree growth forming a mystical, gnarled elfin forest shrouded in mist. Riding through this humid forest can be an eerie experience. As the fog descends over the twisted trees, the mysterious sounds of the rainforest fill the air – the distant roar of howler monkeys, the scurrying of small mammals across the organic forest floor, the mournful call of invisible rainforest birds. Light dapples through the dripping foliage creating a kaleidoscope of green and silver, a jewelled mosaic of light and shade.

After spending a day in this enchanted region, the riders again hit the trail, taking in astonishing views as they begin their descent into the belly of one of the world's most active volcanoes, Arenal. This is a different world again – desolate and starkly beautiful, a lunar landscape created by a massive explosion in 1968.

Leaving their horses at the national park's entrance, the group continues on foot to an eruption site before being transported to the Tabacon Spa to luxuriate in natural hot springs fed by the volcano. This upmarket health spa offers volcanic mud wraps, massages and aromatherapy as well as the reviving power of the thermo-mineral pools. Such indulgence is a rare treat on a horse trek, just one of the unique and special features of this ride in a truly intriguing destination.

The final ecosystem explored on the Odyssey tour is the sprawling savanna of the Guanacaste region, the home of the Costa Rican cowboy. Three-quarters of the country's cattle are bred

in this northern province; it is also great Criollo horse country. However, in keeping with Costa Rica's emphasis on sustainable agriculture, many ranch owners are restoring their land to its natural state, allowing the forests to reclaim their former prominence.

Los Innocente Hacienda covers around 1053ha (2600 acres) of virgin forest, secondary growth forest and grasslands adjoining the Guanacaste National Park. Once used for grazing beef and dairy cattle, it is now held in conservation, providing rich habitat for an amazing array of wildlife, including spider monkeys, white-faced capuchin monkeys, armadillos, iguanas and even sloths. Birdlife is plentiful, a rainbow display as exotic scarlet macaws, parrots and toucans flash through the blue sky.

Fruit trees laden with fruit again entice passing riders – what could be more delicious than a mango freshly plucked and shared with your appreciative mount? In this environment everything seems to taste and smell better; your senses heightened by the incredible beauty, fertility and richness of life in this amazing tropical world – but that's paradise for you!

LEFT *The Sobralia orchid* (Sobralia macrantha) *grows in lava in the Arenal Volcano National Park of Costa Rica.*

ABOVE *Exploring the Monteverde Cloud Forest on foot adds another dimension to an exciting eco-safari on horseback.*

Torres del Paine Vistas

Torres del Paine Vistas

PATAGONIA, CHILE

Location *Torres del Paine National Park*

Getting there *A four-hour transfer from Punta Arenas*

Season *December–March*

Duration *10 days*

Group size *2–12 riders*

Horses *Criollo*

Tack *Chilean*

Pace *Moderate to fast*

Riding ability *Strong intermediate; capable of galloping*

There's a spiritual quality about the granite sculptures standing at heights of 3000m (9843ft), which comprise the Torres del Paine Massif, born about 12 million years ago when the earth was restless. Early settlers in this Patagonian wonderland sensed the magic too. For them, this was the end of the world as they knew it and, on seeing these mountains, they declared: 'At the end of the world, another world begins.' And what a world it is!

You are in the stunning Torres del Paine National Park, Patagonia, Chile. You are riding sturdy and surefooted Criollos, referred to as the Kings of the Pampa, and you are in the care of the Lords of Patagonia – the *baqueanos* – decked in their traditional working garb.

These horses are described as fearless and independent. The Criollo is said to be a one-man horse; it is often very affectionate, but doesn't trust just anybody. Once trust is established, it gives all of itself with amazing courage and tenacity. It fears nothing and goes absolutely anywhere – proof of this was shown along the way.

The *baqueanos* are justifiably proud of their skills and traditions, which extend well past riding. They are said to be serious and reserved gauchos who know twenty thousand square leagues of plain, mountain and wood.

This is one of the most beautiful, unspoiled and remote places on the planet. The Torres del Paine area was pronounced a national park in 1959, and was further declared a biosphere reserve in 1978. It covers 181,000ha (447,251 acres) and

the altitude varies from 50m (164ft) to more than 3000m (9840ft) above sea level. The air is crystal clear and cool, and the park is home to many rare species such as puma, skunk, flamingo, deer, nandu (ostrich), guanaco (smaller relatives of the llama) and red and grey foxes. Presiding over all creatures and hovering with its watchful eye, is the king of the sky, the mighty condor.

Stunning and overwhelming, this world offers few physical comforts to the traveller. Relentless icy winds prevail more often than not; so strong that contact lenses peel off the eyes and unsecured sunglasses fly off into a void. However, the nourishment this world affords the soul is beyond measure, especially the soul of a rider. It smiles!

The 10-day wilderness riding programme starts at Punta Arenas, a true frontier town on the southernmost tip of the South American continent. Here, ships rest at anchor between their voyages to Antarctica, and ferries to Terra del Fuego ply their trade. Monuments of explorers and architecture reminiscent of Spanish, English as well as German colonial times add charm and romance. Of course supermarkets, fast-food outlets and Internet cafés have found their spots too. Very little English is spoken overall, but a smile and mime establishes communications very effectively.

A four-wheel-drive vehicle takes our group of riders 400km (248 miles) north via Puerto Natales – a delightful small town on the shores of Canal Señoret – to Laguna Azul, one of the park's three entry points and the start of our ride.

ABOVE LEFT *Lago Pingo is filled with floating icebergs, which regularly break off from the Pingo Glacier.*

OPPOSITE *Riders slowly make their way over flat, grassy terrain toward Lake Pehoe, en route to the Torres del Paine National Park.*

By late afternoon, which is when we arrived, the clouds had drifted beyond the far end of the lake. Laguna Azul fortunately has a mild microclimate, thus the first night, despite a little rain, was quite comfortable. We readied our tents for the night. All possessions had been packed into deep waterproof stuff sacks before we left Punta Arenas. Now was the test of our packing proficiency; how far down these long tubular packs were the toothbrushes? Half a sheep thrown onto the grill and full-bodied Chilean red wine with dinner ensured that we slept well!

The drumming of hooves woke us early the next morning – the horses had arrived at a gallop! After sunrise the clouds partly cleared and allowed our destination, the magical Torres, to greet us across the lake.

The packhorses are securely loaded, the *baqueanos'* indispensable *maté* leaves are packed inside waterproof calfskins, attached to their saddles. We, the tourists, safely aboard our steeds, embraced the forthcoming adventures with gusto.

Horses eager to go, we set off riding along the shores of Laguna Azul toward the most stunning vista. Snowcapped mountains beyond the lake, a

ABOVE *A riding group prepares to leave the Lake Azul region and progress toward the beckoning Torres, the mountains for which the national park is named.*

OPPOSITE TOP LEFT Baqueano *Chechin, dressed in traditional garb, eagerly waits for his riding group to catch up before the steep descent to Laguna Honda.*

OPPOSITE TOP RIGHT *A wild herd of guanacos, a smaller form of llama, fearlessly observes as riders make their way across the hills of the park. Quite a few herds can be seen in the park.*

glacier tilts toward us. The three slender granite towers, the 'Torres', pierce the blue sky. We looked on in awe and did our best to sit on our horses Chilean style – well back in the saddle with the legs thrust forward. It took some getting used to.

A condor above seemed suspended in midair, pointing toward the Cuernos (Horns) del Paine, as icy winds from glaciers below held him aloft. We reined in our horses and gazed in wonder at the panorama.

Siesta time introduced us to *maté* – a thick stewed tea – and the tradition involved in drink-ing it. We all had a little snooze, including our youngest traveller, a cute eight-month-old foal whose mother was one of our spare riding horses. Just by running along freely like the packhorses, foals learn their job early.

At sunset we reached the banks of a big, fast-flowing river, cooled by a couple of floating ice-bergs which had broken off the Dickson Glacier several miles upstream. One of the *baqueanos* started cracking his whip, the sound carried well across the water and within minutes a man emerged from the trees on the opposite bank. He tightened the rope that spanned the river and

proceeded to haul a rubber dinghy over to us. The horses, stripped of their gear, were chased into the icy waters. With little enthusiasm and much snorting they swam across. The gloveless ferryman skilfully pulled us across, along with all the provisions, with a hand-over-hand action. He had to do seven trips!

On the other side, the *refugio* tucked away in a clearing offers shelter to hikers, canoeists and riders; there is no vehicle access. Cold, damp, tired but happy we entered the wooden cabin.

The offer of a Pisco Sour, the delicious combination of Chilean brandy, egg white, sugar, lemon juice and ice rounded off a perfect day. The horses spent the night grazing free.

We stayed in the national park for another nine wonderful days, leaving its perimeter only for excursions to a puma hunter's sheep farm.

Floor rugs and chair covers at Estancia Tercera attested to many a successful hunt – on the wall, treasured rifles framed a pair of puma-skin chaps.

Pumas, the parks biggest predators, quite frequently attack horses and we saw many bearing the scars of close encounters, as well as a recent kill. The magnificent cats are protected within the park, but hunted elsewhere to ensure the survival of livestock.

Isolation is a way of life in this corner of the world. At the edge of the treeline, close to the base of the Dickson Glacier, surrounded by gnarled and twisted bonsai-like Antarctic beech trees, is a police station – the most remote one on the planet. The lonely guard on duty works seven-day shifts, and the only people he sees are the tourists who come from all over the world to explore his backyard by canoe, boat, car, on foot, or, as we did, on horseback.

He must have the most scenic commute to work – getting flown in and out. We envied his chance to view the majestic mountains (i.e via plane), but he implied that he does not see much, because he is too busy throwing up. The conversation took place mainly by mime.

Accommodation en route was mainly in tents and *refugios* – we also stayed on a small farm hotel, Hosteria Mirador Del Payne, which is located a few meters outside the official central park zone.

TOP *A condor gracefully soars in the blue sky; it is an iconic symbol of this cold and rugged southern wilderness.*
LEFT *Horses swim across the icy-cold waters of Lago Dickson to get to the night's shelter.*

Halfway through our ride we stayed at the latter, and gave our horses a day off by using the animals owned by the hotel. Again, brilliantly safe and good horses took us over the mountain to a shack inhabited by a cattle herder with his three dogs and two horses. He lives there most of the year. The *questo* or shack was made of planks and tin, and had a wood fire in the middle with a cauldron suspended over it. A bed, table, bench and some shelves are the only furniture. A sort of stable door has the bottom half made of timber, but the top half is a side of beef, ready to add slices to the stew.

A few sides of air-dried beef were suspended from a huge tree outside beyond the reach of

ABOVE *A baqueano leads a riding group through the wild pampas with views of the picturesque Sierra del Torro.*

dogs and puma. Too cold for flies, it made the ideal storage. A light dusting of snow, experienced the morning of the visit at the *questo*, added to the magic of the ancient forest.

When we emerged from the trees at about 1100m (3610ft), the Torres 'greeted us' from across the valleys of Lago Sarmiento and Lago Nordenskjold. From this elevated position, we took in the view in silence, totally enraptured by the moment.

As on most days, the distance covered was somewhere between 30 and 40km (19 and 25 miles). Again, we found a stretch of pampas where we could let our horses have free rein and gallop for a few kilometres. They seemed to love this as much as we did.

We followed lively rivers, tranquil waters of lakes green and lakes blue, some with icebergs and others without. We passed through the southernmost forests of the planet, crossed

streams and felt the invigorating vibrancy of this very special place. It was glorious to climb so high that condors appeared within touching distance. We felt very smug after descending long steep slopes of rock and scree. Had the horses baulked even slightly, we would have been only too happy to dismount and slide. But we couldn't let the Criollos down – we felt that our courage should at least match theirs.

We met great people along the way and at the *refugios*. The friendly banter among the dedicated adventurers of all ages, ranged from the experiences of the day to those of past exploits around the globe.

At every chance we got, we nibbled Calafate berries. They grew in large patches and added a touch of colour to the dull grey, rocky ground. Legend has it that once you eat of the berries, you will return to this country. I sincerely hope it's true!

Europe

Glaciers and Deserts of Iceland ✪ Discovering Sligo on Horseback ✪ The Argyll Highlands
Exploring England on Horseback ✪ Exploring the Camargue ✪ The Forests and Beaches of Andalucia
Bridle Trails of Umbria ✪ Csikós of the Puszta ✪ Land of Beautiful Horses

Glaciers and Deserts of Iceland

Glaciers & Deserts of Iceland

REYKJAVÍK REGION, ICELAND

Location *Vellir, near Reykjavík*

Getting there *A 30-minute drive from Reykjavík, transfers included*

Season *July–August*

Duration *2–9 days*

Group size *No limit*

Horses *Icelandic Horse*

Tack *English style; helmets mandatory*

Pace *Moderate with lots of* tölting

Riding ability *Intermediate*

THEY SAY THAT THE MAJORITY OF ICELANDERS STILL believe in elves and trolls, and as we ride through this enchanted landscape, it's easy to understand why. Contorted rock formations are etched with the leering faces of evil trolls and shadows flit supernaturally across black volcanic crevices, the eerie howl of the wind muffling the scurrying of tiny feet. This is an improbable world, a mythical place where the imagination runs riot, where daily life has a fairytale quality dictated by little horses straight from a child's picture book.

Iceland is a land unlike any other on earth, a surrealist work of art inexplicably brought to life. Stark and austere, it is unconventionally beautiful, a moonscape peppered with intense colours and bold shapes as well as dramatic vistas.

In summer, its treeless plains are bathed in the Northern Lights, the constant daylight a powerful presence; while in winter, the land sleeps in eternal darkness. Over half the island is covered by lava fields and deserts dotted with bubbling mud pools and outdoor springs heated by geothermal forces. Geysers spew forth from the belly of the earth, and glaciers sit atop active volcanoes, melting into gushing rivers which carve the rocky surface with the deftness of a sculptor's chisel.

This extraterrestrial island is located in the North Atlantic Ocean on the fringe of the Arctic Circle, remote and distant, yet only a five-hour flight from New York City. Long isolated from the rest of the world, its people are a homogenous race, many of them descendants of the original Viking settlers who arrived around AD900. They still speak an Old Norse dialect, are listed in the telephone directory by their first names, and are renowned for opening up their homes to strangers. Paradoxically, they are also extremely sophisticated with a love of rock music. Iceland is one of the countries with the highest per capita use of cell (mobile) phones and the Internet.

Forty per cent of Iceland's 282,000 citizens live in the capital, Reykjavík, a pretty city with a quaint European style. However, up until a few generations ago, most Icelanders were farmers, their lifestyle pretty much shaped by the land. To truly understand the country, then, it is necessary to travel outside the city, experiencing nature in its raw, untamed state. What better way to explore this island of fire and ice than on the back of its national treasure, the Icelandic Horse?

Small in stature, stocky and sturdy, the delightful Icelandic Horse is, like its people, a creation of Iceland's bizarre landscape – the isolation and extremes of weather and terrain moulding its temperament and unique characteristics.

Its story is indelibly linked to the island's history, which all began at the end of the ninth century. A group of rebellious Norwegian Vikings fled the tyrannical rule of King Harold in open longboats. With them they brought all that was necessary for a new life – their families, supplies and livestock. Among what was deemed worthy were the most precious possessions of all – horses.

From the beginning, the horse played a central role in survival in this harsh land. They were

PREVIOUS PAGES *Horse riding is a good way to explore the Carmague without disrupting its fragile wetlands.*
ABOVE LEFT *The Icelandic Horse is inherently sound and its cute, cuddly appearance makes*

it a favourite among the children of the island.
OPPOSITE *Even at the height of summer, the stark and austere Icelandic landscape can appear bleak and foreboding.*

used for herding sheep, exploring the mountains, as a beast of burden and a companion. With few roads, the horses were the only means of transport over rough, rugged and boggy terrain – even carts could not be utilized. They were used as pack animals, for riding, and as a food source – the most needed servant of all.

In the early days of the Norse settlement, the horse was worshipped as a deity and a symbol of fertility. It was the inspiration for poems, songs and sagas. A good horse was a status symbol, and it was the strongest wish of many horsemen to meet their 'good horse' on the other side of the grave. Even the gods cherished their steeds – Sleipnir, owned by the god Odin, had eight legs and was the fastest horse of all.

In the 12th century, the Icelandic parliament declared a ban on importing horses in order to prevent the outbreak of disease – a law that is still in force today. Nearly a thousand years of isolation since has resulted in one of the purest breeds in the world, one untainted by mixed blood.

Although breeding standards were followed, climatic extremes rather than man-made ideals are responsible for the character and appearance of the Icelandic Horse. Small in stature – only about 13 hands high – it is strong and swift, spirited but reliable, and extremely affectionate. It has a shaggy coat, thick, lustrous mane and tail, dense bone structure and a cute, pony-like head. This horse is famously surefooted, with strong homing instincts and great stamina. The Icelandic also lives to a ripe old age, leading a useful life well into its 30s and 40s. The oldest horse on record was Thulla, an Icelandic mare who died at the age of 57, fading from health only after her elderly owner passed away.

With no natural predators, Icelandic Horses are said to be less responsive to the flight instinct. They have a tendency to work their way around danger. This level-headedness is a prized quality, particularly among trekking horses carrying inexperienced riders.

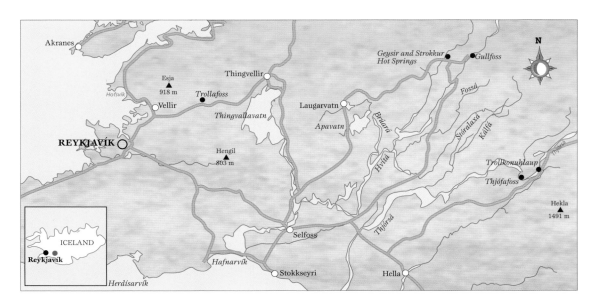

ABOVE LEFT *The Icelandic Horse is a product of its environment; tough, surefooted and strong, yet it is docile with an indomitable spirit.*

What most distinguishes the Icelandic Horse, however, is its unique fifth gait, the *tölt*. This is a kind of running walk; a four-beat gait which allows the horse to literally float over rugged ground, offering a smooth and comfortable ride. The footfalls are back left, front left, back right, and front right. Because there is no suspension phase like the trot or canter, this gait is uncannily silky with no jarring to the rider's back or rear end. This is a fully natural action, and you

ABOVE *Riding with a large herd of free-roaming spare horses adds to the excitement of horse trekking in Iceland.*

can observe young foals *tölting* happily in the paddocks. The rider's position in the saddle with legs thrust down and forward does assist the horse in this gait.

It is on long rides in the countryside where this gait comes into its own; the rider can relax as his horse glides across fields. There is a saying in Iceland that the *tölt* is a true gift from God. Something that few horse trekkers would argue with.

The *tölting* Icelandic Horse is certainly a blessing for the people of Iceland. It is, in fact, one of the major natural resources of the country and the backbone of the nation's tourist industry. There are around 100,000 horses on the island, the highest horses-to-people ratio in the world. Commercial

trekking is a well-established business, and trails are found all across the country. There are numerous horse-riding operators, some of them enormous concerns with over 1000 horses – the largest herds in the world. The rides are seasonal, which run from June through to September, before the long, bleak winter sets in. However, even in midsummer the weather can be unpredictable so riders need to prepare for any extreme, even snow.

Horse touring in Iceland has its roots in common farming practices. During the summer months, sheep farmers would take their horses out for a few days at a time, training them for the hard work of the fall roundups. Accompanying the horses under saddle was a herd of spare horses, the farmer swapping three or four times a day to keep his mounts fresh and willing. On a typical riding day, over 48km (30 miles) might be covered, with the herd moving along at a fair clip to cover the distances.

This practice is now a unique feature of Iceland's commercial riding tours, with people coming from all over the world to participate. Not only is it fun to swap horses, with each horse providing a different experience, but it's also an incredibly kind regime for the animals which is reflected in the Icelandic's willingness to perform. The horse seems to understand that its time under saddle is limited, so it has no qualms about putting in the effort while working. The drive of the Icelandic Horse takes many visitors by surprise – the thundering pace and enthusiasm belying its 'shaggy little pony' appearance.

The experience of *tölting* along with up to 60 other horses running free beside you is a remarkable experience. Sometimes the horses will take advantage of their freedom, disappearing over a hill in an exuberant display; then, just as you think they are lost forever, they reappear, the herd instinct bonding them together.

Most of the commercial operators offer a 'riding with the herd' option, which is recommended only for experienced riders prepared for long hours in the saddle. Eldhestar, the biggest horse-trekking company in Iceland, offers tours from one hour to 10 days, working with up to 2000 horses at nine different locations in Iceland. On the longer tours, three horses are provided for each rider, and guests are encouraged to assist in the driving and care of the herd.

The possibilities for exploration of this island are endless; crossing ancient riding routes from north to south and visiting places which, by their very names, exude mystery – the Waterfall of Thieves, the Elves Church (a giant cave where elves are said to marry), and Trollafoss (the Troll-Woman's Waterfall). There are tours to the northern beaches of the Atlantic, to the eastern climes where you ride alongside herds of reindeer, and through lava fields dotted with hot pools, the ideal place to wind down after a long day in the saddle.

Most of Eldhestar's treks set off from their headquarters, a ranch conveniently located at Vellir, a 30-minute drive from Reykjavík and the perfect location for exploring the varied landscape

of southern Iceland. A tour encompassing the most popular attractions of this region is the Golden Highlights of the South, a classic trek designed to provide the archetypal Icelandic experience of volcanoes, hot springs, geysers and vast treeless plains.

This is a region abounding in history and folklore, and if you don't have much knowledge about Icelandic culture, you soon will as you are bombarded with evocative tales of Viking gods, noble historic events, great heroes and the cheeky antics of elves, fairies and trolls. In this wild and convoluted landscape, it is easy for the imagination to take flight, fact and fantasy blurring into a never-ending story, which, in the context of the scenery, makes perfect sense.

After riding across the moors surrounding Vellir, the Golden Highlights ride crosses lava fields formed in the year 1000 when the volcano Hengill blew its top. As legend has it, this was an act of revenge by three warring gods: Thor, Olin and Freyr. Beyond lies the original meeting place of the Althing, Iceland's legislative assembly and the oldest continually operating parliament in Europe. Momentous decisions have been made at

this site. In the year 1000, the Althing voted to adopt Christianity; and 200 years later, the parliament voted to give up its independence to the Norwegian crown. It was also an important site for the Icelandic Horse. Here, the purity of the breed was guaranteed when the government declared a ban on the importation of other horses.

Continuing past mountains and lakes, lava fields and hot springs, the ride progresses to one of Iceland's great sites, the hot springs of Geysir. The original geyser, the one for which all other waterspouts are named, no longer flows; but the nearby Strokkur spout goes off with clockwork regularity, its 18m (60ft) projectile spout entertaining and astounding all visitors.

The ride pushes on at a steady *tölting* pace, past one of Iceland's most beautiful waterfalls, Gullfoss, or the Golden Falls. In summer, the double-tiered fall often has a spectacular double rainbow above; in winter, it freezes midstream, an incredible sight for the few visitors who brave the subzero temperatures.

Beyond Gullfoss, tourists become rare as you travel along icy river banks and through silent highlands abounding in legend. At Thjófafoss – the Waterfall of Thieves – the story is told of a band of petty thieves punished for their crimes by drowning. Nearby, the Trollkonuhlaup – the Giantess Waterfall – was named after a giantess, a large and enterprising lass who threw boulders into the river so she could cross to the other side without getting wet.

The stories keep coming, hours of entertainment over wholesome meals of baked salmon and a warm drink at the end of each day's ride.

Accommodation en route is in keeping with the landscape; austere and rustic in simple mountain huts, quaint guesthouses and community centres. The occasional lack of facilities, however, is more than compensated for by the presence of numerous hot springs, arguably the most popular feature of the Iceland rides.

Here, soaking in the steaming pools, surrounded by the ghostly black crevices of ancient lava flows and a spectacular backdrop of towering glacial mountains, you begin to appreciate the special meaning of this geological wonderland. This is a place to absorb not only the healing warmth of the waters, but also the wonderful stories of this fascinating fairyland and its magical horses.

OPPOSITE *Locals have relied on Icelandic Horses for generations, now the trekking industry finds them useful too.*

ABOVE *Icelandic Horses are kept in a semiferal state and can endure severe winter conditions and difficult mountainous country.*

Discovering Sligo on Horseback

Sligo on Horseback
SLIEVE PENINSULA, IRELAND

Location *Donegal Bay, Sligo*

Getting there *Flight to Sligo airport*

Season *April–November*

Duration *8 days, 7 nights*

Group size *Minimun of 2; maximum of 6 riders*

Horses *Irish Hunter, Connemara*

Tack *English; helmets recommended*

Pace *Moderate*

Riding ability *Strong intermediate; independant riding skills necessary*

A HORSE WALKS INTO AN IRISH PUB AND ORDERS a drink. The barman gives him one. The horse complains loudly, 'Hey, what sort of a barman are you! You forgot the little umbrella!' He finishes his drink and gallops out of the bar. After the horse has left, another customer, who has been watching the whole scene with increasing astonishment, turns to the barman and says, 'That is incredible! I have never seen anything like that before, never in my entire life!' The barman replies: 'What's the big deal! Anyone can forget the little umbrella!'

If there are three things the Irish know well, it's humour, drinking and horses. The fact that all three come together so frequently is no surprise – horses are as much a part of the Irish experience as Guinness, leprechauns and the vagaries of the weather. There are horses everywhere on the Emerald Isle – in the lush green pastures, pulling carts and caravans, trotting down country lanes, and on racetracks and sporting arenas, a dominion where the Irish horse reigns supreme. And yes, it's not uncommon to see a horse in a pub, sharing a refreshing pint with its owner.

An old Irish proverb states, 'Sell the cow, buy the sheep, but never be without the horse.' This sentiment is also extended to Ireland's visitors, with the Irish Tourist Board heavily promoting horse-riding holidays in conjunction with a proactive and well-organized alliance of Irish equestrian centres called Horse Riding Ireland.

There is probably nowhere in the world that caters so readily to the international horse-riding populace. There are many opportunities for trail riding, cross-country jumping and dressage, all combined into affordable and enticing holiday packages including accommodation, horse hire and tuition. Some establishments, such as Ballycormac House in Tipperary, even offer guests the opportunity to compete in local fairs and show-jumping competitions, including the International Dublin Horse Show. During the hunting season, which lasts from late October to mid-March, guests also have the chance to experience fox hunting on Ballycormac's team of gallant jumpers.

The terrain covered on Irish treks is as varied as the riding disciplines; from the legendary wilds of Connemara with its moody landscape and famous white ponies to the picture-perfect Ring of Kerry, or the grandeur of the Wicklow Trail. Ireland's scenery is one designed to soothe the soul with its soft mists, emerald pocket-handkerchief-sized fields, quaint villages and deserted beaches offering a little corner of horse-riding heaven.

In the words of Judie Framan, 'We rode into the mountains for hours without encountering other people. Pearlized mist hung over the top of the peaks, giving them a magical glow. One moment we were riding along in sunshine, then clouds rolled overhead and a gentle misty rain began to fall. Sometimes a blackened sky threatened a downpour. Thus we learned about Irish weather. It is what it is – the rain, morning mist and cool temperatures are all integral to making Ireland a fantasy in green…'

ABOVE LEFT *Riders slow down the pace to take in the captivating sunset over Donegal Bay. A peaceful end to a day of exploring the countryside.*

OPPOSITE *Dressed in warm jackets to guard against cold weather, a group of riders sets out to trek in Ireland.*

One of the most beautiful and untouched parts of the Irish Republic is Sligo, a county immortalized by the famous Irish poet William Butler Yeats. Here, in the shadow of the flat-topped Ben Bulben, overlooking the shimmering shores of Donegal Bay and the Slieve Peninsula is Horse Holiday Farm, one of Ireland's leading equestrian centres where experienced and independent riders are given the opportunity to try something really different – an unguided trail ride.

This is how it works. After a mandatory assessment to establish riding ability, guests are given their own horse for the week, a map and specific instructions on how to find their accommodation. They are then left to their own devices, exploring the countryside at their own pace. Every night, there is a warm bed and a hearty meal waiting at a prearranged bed-and-breakfast establishment, where you'll also find a field and fodder for your horse. You are provided with all the equipment for your horse, which include tack, grooming equipment and emergency provisions, as well as saddlebags for your personal luggage, and advice on how best to experience this country.

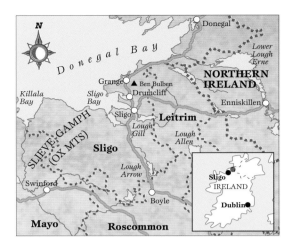

There is a real sense of freedom in this sort of travel, but it demands independence and more than a touch of bravery. It's as close to owning your own horse as possible; in fact, many riders overcome with emotion are reluctant to part with their new-found friend, buying their horses at the end of their week's vacation.

While some travellers may feel trepidation at the thought of riding off on a strange horse in unfamiliar territory, the warmth and effusive hospitality of the Irish people makes it an easy and pleasurable experience. Each night, you are

welcomed by your hosts as a long-lost friend, fed to exploding point, and spoiled rotten before being sent on your way the following morning with yet another full belly, courtesy of a hearty Irish breakfast. The inevitable task of asking for directions becomes an invitation for a chat about the two Irish obsessions – weather and horses. While en route, the prospect of a refreshing drink, a warming fire and good *craic* makes a visit to a local pub an integral part of the experience.

While new friendships are forged over a pint of Guinness, the strongest bond is formed with the real stars of this equine show, the horses of Horse Holiday Farm. Beautiful, strong and willing, many of them are bred and raised on the farm by German-born owner Tilman Anhold, a man with an uncanny knack for matching horse and rider.

Tilman's horses are mainly Irish Hunters, a cross between a Thoroughbred stallion and an Irish Draught mare. Dating back to Celtic times, the Irish Draught is a horse famed for its strength, docility and strong constitution. Lighter than most European draft breeds, it was the backbone of the Irish rural economy as it was expected not only to work on the farm, but also to fulfil riding duties. When crossed with the modern Thoroughbred, a breed that also thrives on the verdant Irish pastures, the result is an attractive, strong-boned horse that is robust, level headed and an outstanding competitor in any sporting event.

Ridden on a loose rein, Tilman's horses step out with surefooted confidence over all kinds of terrain, from boggy peat to cobbled lanes. It is on the wonderful sandy beaches of the Atlantic coast, however, that these horses come into their own, their agility and speed soon apparent.

According to *The Rider's ABC* – an amusing tome of rules provided by Horse Holiday Farm – the beach is the horse's 'racetrack', a place where they are allowed to have free rein in a joyful, boisterous gallop. 'As soon as the animals feel the sand under their feet they are transformed and behave more lively, fresher and more sparkling than ever,' it states. 'After many years of training, the animals are used to

taking off. Mostly, they are quite successful with this; the riders shout and cheer with pleasure and encourage the horses even more...'

With pounding hooves, crashing surf, the rush of salty air and the surge of adrenaline, the beach rides are inevitably the most popular feature of the Sligo rides, a rare and exciting experience enjoyed by both horse and rider. There are literally kilometres (miles) of deserted beaches to explore along hard-packed sand flats battered by enormous waves, and through an extensive dune system of soft sand and grasses. Depending on the tides, you can even ride out to offshore Dernish Isle, where you can view seal families basking on sandbanks and rocks.

On the seven-day Sligo trail ride, three full days are spent on the coastline with the remainder of the trip exploring the hills, lakes and villages of Counties Sligo and Leitrim, along small lanes and through forests, past castles and historic houses. An ever-visible presence is Ben Bulben, the flat-topped table mountain which has become the symbol of Sligo, and a site of pilgrimage for Yeats fans who come to view the landform that inspired his most famous poem: 'Under bare Ben Bulben's head... In Drumcliff churchyard Yeats is laid...'

True to his request, Yeats is buried in the parish graveyard at Drumcliff, a tiny village between Grange and Sligo. His self-penned epitaph is curious and chilling: 'Cast a cold eye on life, on death. Horseman, pass by.' The horseman in reference is not a visitor from Horse Holiday Farm, but a figure from local legend, a ghostly Sligo rider who takes the souls of the wicked to hell.

With such dark thoughts, it is comforting to find refuge in one of the warm and welcoming drinking establishments scattered along the Sligo Trail. The Irish pub is more than just a bar, it is an unofficial community centre, a place for entertainment, company and good cheer. One of the pubs near Horse Holiday Farm is

LEFT *Unguided trail rides are ideal for independent riders who have much confidence in their horses and their own navigational skills.*

even a general store selling meat, cheese, butter, milk, eggs and all manner of pharmaceuticals. As *The Rider's ABC* points out, you can do your shopping here until the evening hours, and savour a pint on the side. 'This is why even the men in Ireland volunteer to go shopping.'

Further references to Yeats abound on the Sligo trail, from the historic estate of Lissadell where he stayed on many occasions to the picturesque views of Lough Gill and the lake isle of 'Innisfree', which he immortalized in verse. The Sligo Trail takes you past some beautiful places on the shore of the lake, the perfect place for a picnic or a quiet moment of contemplation.

Although he never lived permanently in Sligo, Yeats was a regular visitor during his childhood years; its inlets, misty meadows and waterfalls inspiring him until his death in 1939. 'I longed for a sod of earth from some field that I knew,' he wrote, 'something of Sligo to hold in my hand.'

ABOVE *Dawn breaks over Lough Gill, promising another perfect day on horseback exploring the beaches and fields of Sligo.*
OPPOSITE *The Connemara Pony, with its strong and sturdy build, distinctive grey coat and gentle nature, is an icon in Ireland.*

Visitors to the Horse Holiday Farm will certainly appreciate this timeless sentiment. 'Memories of riding in Ireland are coloured green and grey, a land of emerald fields and ancient mossy walls lining narrow country lanes. The sounds remembered are those of music, laughter, short and long tales, thundering hoofs along with the sounds of the sea. Country pubs built of stone, great food and hospitality, and excellent whisky to soothe away sore spots! The weather can be as changeable as a leprechaun's mood – three seasons in one day – no problem begorra. One seems to ride into history; it certainly brings out the romantic.' Nelly Gelich couldn't have described it more accurately.

The Argyll Highlands

The Argyll Highlands

ARGYLL REGION, SCOTLAND

Location *Ardrishaig, West Highlands*

Getting there *Own transport or a two-hour transfer from Glasgow Airport*

Season *April–October; shorter trails year round*

Duration *6–7 days*

Group size *Minimum of 2 riders*

Horse *Irish Draught, cobs, native ponies*

Tack *English; helmets mandatory*

Pace *Varies according to trail*

Riding ability *Novice to strong intermediate*

STORM CLOUDS GATHER OVER THE DESOLATE HILLTOPS, ominous, brooding, nature's furrowed brow. In the distance, thunder signals that the weather is about to break, a low rumble reverberating through the earth's surface. The rumble becomes a roar, intensifying; and as a row of riders appears over the crest of a hill, the thunder becomes the pounding of hooves, a victory charge of unbridled power and speed. We gallop over tussocks and bound across boggy ditches, our horses snorting with exertion and the exhilaration of the race, a joyful celebration of freedom in a wild and rugged landscape.

This is Scotland, land of the brave – a tiny country of mythical proportions whose people are fiercely independent, individualistic and proud. Shaped by a violent and turbulent history, it is a country with a rich culture and romantic traditions which are as strongly adhered to today as they were in the days of legendary heroes such as Rob Roy, Robert the Bruce and Mary Queen of Scots.

This is a land where the ghosts of the past haunt a landscape of spectacular beauty, a rugged panorama of sweeping moors and mist-covered mountains, sparkling lochs and peaceful glens. Wild and remote, much of the highland region is inaccessible to vehicles, so the only way to experience it intimately is on horseback, the traditional means of transport in this terrain.

This is great riding country – open, unrestricted with few fences or vestiges of civilization to slow the pace. While the ground can be quite rugged, the tough Scot horses and riders take it all in their stride, travelling fearlessly across streams, up mountains, through forests and over stone walls. Both seem to possess an ingrained spirit of adventure and courage, bred into them over generations, characteristics of survival in such a wild and woolly environment.

Scotland is actually the home of pony trekking, the term originating over 50 years ago as a way of encouraging young people to explore the Scottish countryside on strong, safe, native highland ponies. Today, this is a popular activity with teenagers and inexperienced adult riders who like to travel at a leisurely pace, enjoying the sensational Scottish scenery.

For a more vigorous ride, the terminology to look out for is 'trail riding', which indicates a longer, faster trek into remote and otherwise inaccessible countryside. These are more suitable for experienced riders who are comfortable and secure at all paces, and don't mind the challenge of long hours in the saddle.

A rollicking pace on fit and energetic horses is the signature of one of the United Kingdom's leading equestrian centres, Brenfield Farm, located in the West Highlands village of Ardrishaig. Brenfield is the home of Argyll Trail Riding and Castle Riding Centre, run by Norwegian-born Tove Gray-Stephens and her son David Hay-Thorburn, both respected horse trainers and superb riders.

This Riding Centre has something for everyone, from one-hour hacks to weeklong trails on a versatile team of well-schooled and experienced horses ranging from children's ponies to hunters

ABOVE LEFT *The face of the Highlands – David Hay-Thorburn with his piebald mare Mhairi and a couple of canine companions.*

OPPOSITE *The Loch and Forest Trail takes a scenic route along the shores of Loch Fyne, a trail suitable for all standards of riders.*

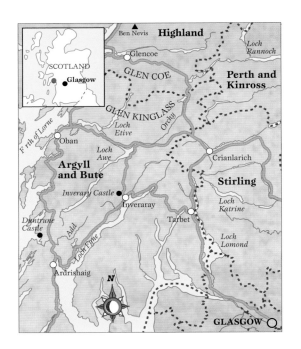

and eventers. Rides either take place in the area immediately surrounding the farm – over kilometres of private farmland, traffic-free forestry and open hillsides with views of nearby Loch Fyne – or beyond, into the heart of the highlands with its remote mountains, historic castles and picturesque deserted beaches.

There are three distinct trails to explore – the Loch and Forest Trail, an easy ride along ancient droving roads into the undiscovered forests of Argyllshire; the Wild Boar Trail, a barnstorming trek for competent riders which includes some sensational beach riding; and the Rob Roy Trail, a 200km (124-mile) test of endurance following in the footsteps of one of Scotland's legendary figures, Rob Roy MacGregor.

Leading the pace is a modern-day local hero, David Hay-Thorburn, a colourful Scottish character with an intimate knowledge and overwhelming passion for his homeland. An excellent horseman, David was the 2000 World Champion of the increasingly popular equestrian sport of Le Trec – orienteering on horseback, and outdoor riding skills.

Le Trec, or *Techniques de Randonner Equestrien de Compétition*, originated in France more than 25 years ago as a way of testing guides working

ABOVE *Trail riding in the Scottish Highlands leads equestrians off the beaten track into the wild and evocative landscape of local heroes.*

in equestrian tourism; the activity soon spread beyond professionals, however, and is now a competitive sport on the continent. The idea is to test a horse and rider's ability to find their way across country using map-reading skills and controlled riding methods. These are the skills needed to cope with the sort of problems which would be encountered when riding alone in remote countryside.

Navigation through mountainous territory comes naturally to David Hay-Thorburn; after

RIGHT *In the Scottish lexicon, 'pony trekking' refers to a sedate ride on trustworthy Highland ponies in a scenic location.*

stately homes and churches all tell the story of a notorious past filled with battles, family feuds and struggles for independence. The most infamous local figure was Rob Roy MacGregor, an outlaw, rebel and cattle rustler who became a folk hero, a latter-day Robin Hood who was a legend in his own lifetime.

Rob MacGregor was born in 1671, his fiery red hair earning him the nickname of Rob Ruadh (Gaelic for 'red'), which was later anglicized into Rob Roy. A supporter of the Jacobite cause, Rob Roy's life of infamy began after his family was evicted and his lands seized by the Duke of Montrose. Rob Roy sought revenge, starting a campaign of cattle rustling, theft and banditry. Gradually, his vendetta became one against all landed gentry who were not prepared to pay him to 'protect' their stock and property.

Despite having a price on his head, Rob Roy had influential supporters, including the Duke of Argyll, a long-standing enemy of Montrose. In 1723, Daniel Defoe wrote of Rob Roy's exploits in *Highland Rogue*; and in 1726, Rob Roy received a Royal Pardon by public acclaim.

Like all good folk heroes, Rob Roy was embraced by his homeland after his death in 1734, his infamy expanding with the publication

all, that's what he does every day on his highland treks! David's partner is an equally colourful character – the splashy piebald Irish cob mare, Mhairi, whose loud markings, wall eyes, heavy build and feathered feet make quite a statement on the international competitive circuit!

Of course, the best training for this sort of competition is out in the wilds, which the Argyll region has in abundance. The Brenfield horses are exposed to the full gamut of challenges – peaty bogs, steep mountain sides, fast-flowing rivers and dizzying passes. High levels of fitness, common sense and steady feet are a prerequisite; for this reason, Brenfield uses a lot of native British Isle horses, such as Irish cobs, Irish Draught crosses, and local Highland ponies – horses which have been bred to handle such extremes.

If there's one thing the Brenfield horses love, it's a fast gallop along the shores of Loch Fyne, followed by a bracing swim. The horses hit the water running, the impetus driving them into the water. They continue the galloping motion as the depth of the water slows the pace; then, as they reach the shallows, the horses once again start to canter as their hooves touch the

sand below. The swim finishes with an exhilarating gallop to the opposite side.

Naturally, this is a pretty soggy activity in a part of the world not renowned for its beach climate! The horses wear specially made webbing bridles, and the saddles are synthetic, with a waterproof cover. As for the riders, they are donned in waterproof trousers, worn over jodhpurs and taped to the top of knee-high rubber riding boots – no bikinis and bare feet here!

Swimming horses, for those who have never tried it before, is quite a surreal experience! The horses are ridden on a loose rein, given free rein so that they can stretch out and find their footing. The riders must wrap their legs tightly around the saddle, feet pushing slightly forward against the current, and one hand clutching the mane as extra support.

There are several opportunities to swim the horses on the Wild Boar Trail, a 241km (150-mile) six-day journey across the Western Highlands. The most exciting experience is at the estuary of the River Add – a 6km (four-mile) gallop and swim towards Duntrune Castle standing, sentry-like, on the opposite headland. This part of Scotland is a history devotee's nirvana – castles,

---

TOP *The thrill of galloping through the shallows of Loch Fyne is one of the highlights of the Wild Boar trail ride.*

RIGHT *Highland ponies are sturdy and reliable riding companions, bred to endure the harsh winters of the mountains.*

ABOVE *Brenfield's Rob Roy Trail sets off from Inveraray Castle, a significant landmark in the legend of Rob Roy MacGregor.*

of Sir Walter Scott's novel 'Rob Roy' in 1818. He has since been the subject of verse, fiction and film; and in 2002, a long-distance walking track called the Rob Roy Way was established to link the places that featured in his colourful life.

Brenfield's Rob Roy Trail sets off from the ground of Inveraray Castle, the seat of the Duke of Argyll himself, heading north up the picturesque Glen Shira. Nearby is Rob Roy's hideout, where he lived under the protection of Argyll after Montrose and the English troops destroyed his house.

The trail crosses bogs and lakes, up mountains and into verdant glens, tough going which can create quite a thirst! Naturally, a 'wee dram' is on the agenda, the fine Scotch whisky provide sustenance for the next leg of the journey.

The following day takes the Brenfield riding group across the river Orchy and through forests, riding along old drover's roads where that scoundrel Rob Roy and his clansmen ran their 'protection racket', charging cattle herders for safe passage.

The longest day in the saddle travels through Glen Kinglass – wild, evocative heather-strewn country which is home to deer and rare birds of prey. This is a lovely, challenging ride with river crossings and ditches to keep both horses and riders on their toes. The destination of this 35km (22-mile) journey is the remote and beautiful Loch Etive, a place of sanctuary for both the native wildlife and the hooligan rogues of the past.

After a peaceful night's sleep in one of the comfortable hotels utilized en route, the trail continues through the deep ravine of Lairig Gartain before scaling the snow-covered peak of Buachille Etive Beag, climbing 366m (1200ft) in just over an hour. This is the head of historic Glen Coe, the site of the infamous McDonald massacre in 1692 and, yet another reminder of Scotland's bloody past.

The Rob Roy Trail culminates with a ride beneath the shadow of Ben Nevis, the highest mountain in the United Kingdom. This is Scotland at its wildest – remote and fiercely beautiful, beloved by photographers but rarely experienced in the flesh.

We riders, however, are a privileged few – able to go beyond the tarmac into an untamed world of rare majesty and absolute solitude. Under the steam of our reliable and trusty mounts, we become not just visitors and observers, but part of the landscape, an integral part of its long and fascinating history.

Exploring England on Horseback

Exploring England on Horseback
CUMBRIA, ENGLAND

Location *Sedbergh, Cumbria*

Getting there *Flight to Manchester or Carlisle, or by train to Oxenholme*

Season *May–October*

Duration *2–3 days, longer trips by arrangement*

Group size *Minimum of 2; maximum of 6 riders*

Horses *Welsh Cob*

Tack *English; helmets mandatory*

Pace *Moderate*

Riding ability *Intermediate*

I PLACED MY FOOT IN THE STIRRUP, SWUNG INTO THE saddle and, while gathering the reins I gazed around me in astonishment. I have never been there before, yet the scene before me was so familiar, it felt like home. Cobblestones resounded with the clatter of neatly shod hooves, the avenues of stables lined with Wellington boots, the velvet crash caps and the tweed jackets – I have seen it, experienced it somewhere in the recesses of my imagination. It felt as if I was transported back in time to the pages of my beloved childhood pony novels, to a place where I first fell in love, a vision that has shaped my very being.

For me, this is where it all began – the England of gymkhanas, naughty ponies, baggy jodhpurs, blue ribbons, snooty riding instructors, and the wild, wild moors. This is the horse world that first captured my imagination 30 years ago and determined my future. Everything I knew about horses, my complete knowledge of riding and equestrian life, was based on what I had read in those English books. It was a world I dreamed about, longed for, strove toward – a fictional paradise that has now, a lifetime later, become reality.

For most pony lovers from the Western world, England is a riding Mecca. It is the ultimate horse society with deep-rooted equestrian traditions, disciplined instruction and well-trained horses as well as classic scenery. A visit to one of its many riding establishments is more than just a dream vacation – it is a pilgrimage, a salute to a place that fuelled childhood dreams.

For such an urbanized and densely populated country, horses remain a way of life in England; riding opportunities are readily available. Unfortunately, however, many commercial stables are located in popular tourist regions and cater exclusively to children and beginners, so research beforehand is strongly advised. Also, beware of language quirks. For instance, in some regions of the UK, 'trekking' means a short nose-to-tail excursion for novices, while 'trail riding' involves long-distance riding at a variety of paces designed for more experienced equestrians.

Once your riding needs are established, the decision on where to ride will depend largely on your expectations of scenery. For such a small country, England offers a diversity of locations from the wild and woolly moors of Cornwall to the highlands bordering Scotland. There are the classic areas that evoke romance – Dartmoor, with its gentle woodland scenery; New Forest, the hunting grounds of aristocracy; the cottages and country lanes of Cotswold; and the high heather moorland and ancient oak forests of Exmoor, home to the wild Exmoor pony. In the north, poetic scenes of lakes and snowcapped peaks abound in the beautiful Lakes District, while just outside of London in the Norwich district, you can take a riding tour through history based at a stately Jacobean mansion.

A classic riding destination for overseas and local riders alike is the bleak, treeless expanse of Dartmoor, which offers 777km² (300sq. miles) of unfettered riding country. This is a landscape of many moods, from misty moors to stormy granite tors, panoramic vistas and picturesque carpets of gorse and heather.

ABOVE LEFT *The gentle beauty of the Cumbrian countryside evokes the fictional perfection of pony novels and childhood dreams.*

OPPOSITE *An impeccably turned-out trekking group sets off through the countryside of the Cotswolds, a favourite hacking destination.*

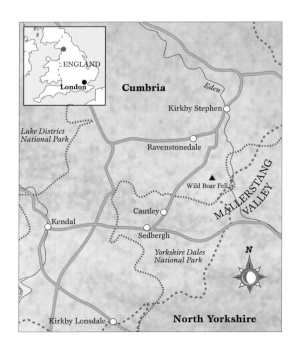

This region presents challenging riding, with delightful, playful native ponies.

One of the most evocative locations in England is the Yorkshire Dales, a place famed for its wide open spaces and warm hospitality. This is the countryside so beautifully captured in James Herriot's *All Creatures Great and Small* – it is a delightful watercolour of quaint rural hamlets, isolated farms and endearing country characters. It is also the world of the Brontë sisters, with its wild and moody moors, stormy skies, and the ghosts of a tragic past.

'I sought, and soon discovered, the three head-stones on the slope next to the moor: the middle one grey, and half buried in heath; Edgar Linton's only harmonized by the turf, and moss creeping up its foot: Heathcliff's still bare. I lingered round them, under that benign sky: watched the moths fluttering among the heath and hare-bells; listened to the soft wind breathing through the grass; and wondered how anyone could ever imagine un-quiet slumbers for the sleepers in that quiet earth.'

EMILY BRONTË, *WUTHERING HEIGHTS*

With such a rich literary tradition, it is hard not to be inspired by the magnificent scenery of the Fells and Dales, even more so when experienced

ABOVE *A deserted country lane in Cumbria flanked by open fields gives horses and riders the opportunity to pick up the pace, while enjoying the unspoiled beauty of the countryside.*

on horseback. This is the perfect location for trekking through unspoiled and impeccably clean countryside, which also presents the opportunity for some heart-thumping, fast-paced riding.

The base for this ride is Low Haygarth Farm in Cautley, Sedbergh, home of D & P Equestrian Enterprises run by the congenial and friendly Barbara Burton. Strategically located midway between the Lakes District and the Yorkshire Dales National Park, the farm is set in a picturesque valley surrounded by the grassy domes of the Howgill Fells. These butte-shaped hills offer extensive views from the Lakes District mountains in the west to the colourful Pennines in the east.

Despite its wild feeling, this is a managed landscape shaped by the hands of man over generations. People have made a living here for over 10,000 years, leaving their mark in the form of ancient settlement sites, monasteries and Roman-built roads. Later, the Vikings settled the region – the Norse heritage reflected in local terminology such as fell (mountain), and dale (valley).

Man-made features dot the landscape – dry stone walls, barns and stone villages – blending harmoniously with the austere landscape and enhancing the ambience of timelessness and solitude. The ancient walls separate countless sheep, the backbone of the economy; yet above the cultivated margins, the fells have been left to nature with the hills cleft by deep ravines, limestone cliffs and spectacular waterfalls. There is virtually no tree cover, but in autumn the springy limestone pasture is blanketed in a sheet of purple heather.

This is as far from the madding crowd as it can possibly get in England, with the area often overlooked by tourists due to the popularity and proximity of the Lakes District. The area tends to be visited only by keen English walkers and locals who recognize the distinctive character of the Howgill Fells and appreciate their quiet solitude. In keeping with the tranquillity of this special

ABOVE RIGHT *Bridle paths through forests and reserves provide an opportunity for horses to stretch out at a canter.*

region, the horse trekking groups of D & P Equestrian are kept small and intimate, with a maximum of six riders at a time. It only takes a couple of days to fully explore the area. On horseback, you can see a lot in a short period, with more than four different types of scenery covered in a day. Riders need to be competent and fit. This is open riding country, inviting a spirited pace, and peppered with tricky ups, downs and river crossings.

Enjoying this classic 'up fell and down dale' experience as much as their riders, is Barbara Burton's team of reliable Welsh Cobs, horses

which are praised for their quality and eagerness. These large-boned, handsome animals are between 14 and 16 hands, impeccably groomed and cared for, and beautifully trained at the farm. Many of them are homebred; all are hand-picked and chosen for their even temperaments.

The most popular rides offered by D & P Equestrian are their multi-day rides, which include lodging at a charming 17th-century former coach house, the Fat Lamb Country Inn. Overseas visitors and the British alike will relish this quaint piece of Yorkshire history with its

friendly, informal atmosphere, great food and eccentric Yorkshire characters with their quirky accents and sense of humour. The inn is set in magnificent countryside bordering its own nature reserve with panoramic views of the fells.

With the vagaries of English weather, it's reassuring to know that at the end of the day there is a hearty meal, a stiff drink and a cozy warm bed to collapse into in preparation for the next day's adventure. This 'down time' is the perfect complement to the riding experience itself, with good food, good company and local tales and legends adding to the flavour of the location.

For romantics, the rewards come early on this delightful trek. Low Haygarth Farm is straight out of a postcard, a white-washed building covered in climbing vines with dry-stone walls, grazing Fell ponies and a moody sky. The overall impression is of perfection – well-groomed, fit horses with perfectly pulled tails; exquisite saddlery impeccably cleaned; neat gardens; pristine villages; happy, cheerful passers-by.

The opportunity to give the horses free rein comes early in the three-day Wild Boar Fell ride, with the beautiful Smardale Nature Reserve inviting a trot through the trees followed by an adrenaline-pumping gallop up the nearby fell. At the top of every hill there is a vista unencumbered by trees, buildings or pollution, a perfect opportunity to be still and soak up the atmosphere of this timeless part of England.

After a night of hearty cheer at the Fat Lamb, the ride continues the following morning through Cote Moor to the Clouds Rock, an unusual area of fissured limestone known as 'pavements'. This is just one of the many limestone features of the area – there are also underground caves, scars, sinkholes and dramatic waterfalls which formed when the area was a tropical sea, and eroded over millions of years by glacial ice.

Just as intriguing are the human remains visited on this ride, including the eerie turreted ruins of Pendragon Castle, said to have been the home

LEFT *Dramatic rock formations are a feature of the Yorkshire Dales region, a wild and intriguing location for horse trekkers.*

of Uther Pendragon, the father of the legendary King Arthur. The ruins date from the 12th century – later, the building was bought and partially restored by Lady Anne Clifford, an indomitable woman who personally saved many of the area's castles and churches in the 17th century.

Pendragon Castle is located in the beautiful Mallerstang Valley. The river Eden flows close by, and above is the forbidding Wild Boar Fell, after which the ride is named. It is said that this mountain was so named because Sir Richard Musgrave of Hartley Castle killed the last wild boar in Westmoreland. A more entertaining story, perhaps, is that of a monk renowned for preaching dull sermons, who was attacked by a wild boar as he crossed the fell. To save his life, he thrust the parchments containing his sermon down the boar's throat, causing the poor creature to die of thirst!

This impressive mountain is obviously one to inspire tall tales and true; and as you gaze at the wild and magnificent panorama which unfolds from the peak of the mountain, it becomes clear why this region has inspired so many poets and authors over the generations.

In the words of JB Priestley, 'In all my travels I have never seen a countryside to equal in beauty the Yorkshire Dales….'

ABOVE *This hilly landscape is home to herds of Fell ponies, one of Britain's most hardy, and popular native breeds.*

RIGHT *Surefooted trekking horses pick their way 'down dale', the vast green moorland stretching before them.*

Exploring the Camargue

Exploring the Camargue
CAMARGUE, SOUTHERN FRANCE

Location *Les Saintes Maries de la Mer*

Getting there *Flight to Montpellier*

Season *Scheduled rides in April, June and September*

Duration *7 days*

Group size *Maximum of 8 riders*

Horses *Camargue Horse (local breeding stock)*

Tack *Local Western style*

Pace *Varied according to conditions*

Riding ability *Moderate to experienced; riders must be competent*

MORE THAN TWENTY YEARS AGO, I SET OFF ON my first great overseas jaunt with two burning ambitions – to visit the countryside which had inspired Van Gogh, and to ride a Camargue Horse. At the time, I had no idea that both dreams would be fulfilled within a day, nor that these two experiences in the Provence region would present such contrasting views of the French countryside.

With its sun-kissed olive groves, shady pine forests and fields of lavender, Van Gogh would not have had to look far beyond his window for inspiration. Yet I can't help but wonder if he ever ventured over the cypress-lined hills of Arles where the River Rhône trickles into the Mediterranean in a wild, lunar landscape of shallow lagoons and salty marshlands. This is the Camargue, a different kind of artistry – a watery wilderness, pink and grey, inhabited by herds of roaming black bulls, legendary white horses and men fuelled by the spirit of gypsies…

And so another tick on my list of 'must do's' – a trail ride on the creature that had inspired my childhood fantasies, the wild 'white horse of the sea'.

Sadly, this particular ride failed to live up to my expectations – my memories are of despondent, dirty ponies plodding nose-to-tail, barely raising the energy to trot along a jam-packed beachfront, and riders swatting desperately at merciless killer mosquitoes intent on devouring our flesh.

Ignorance, insufficient research and a lack of information had led me into a trap common to many tourist resorts around the world – an unfulfilling trail ride aimed at children, novices and suckers! Difficult as it may be to believe, not all horse people are reputable or responsible; there are far too many dishonest operators whose only aim is to make a quick dollar at the expense of clients and horses alike.

It's a case of rider beware – however, there are numerous wonderful horse-riding opportunities in France, including an excellent tour of the Camargue – you just need to know where to find them. The Internet is a great resource and the obvious place to commence your travel research, while specialist horse-riding agencies are an invaluable source of advice, information and assurances of quality.

In terms of organization, infrastructure and quality, France is actually considered one of the premier riding destinations in the world. There are well-organized tours available in every region exploring small villages and walled towns, riding through vineyards, forests and the hunting grounds of magnificent chateaux. The countryside is peaceful and unspoiled, the pace decadently relaxed, and the famous French wine and regional specialties tempt riders to rest, linger and savour. This really is a horse-riding heaven; an indulgence that is as good for the mind and soul as it is for the body!

A couple of tours stand out for their exquisite scenery and riding potential. In the Loire Valley in Central France you can live the life of a pre-Revolutionary aristocrat, riding from castle to castle and being pampered on a grand scale in

ABOVE LEFT *The Camargue Horse is an ancient European breed, its distinctive white coat an adaptation to its watery environment.*

OPPOSITE *Local* gardians *race their spirited horses through the town gates during an* Abrivado *fiesta, the annual 'running of the bulls'.*

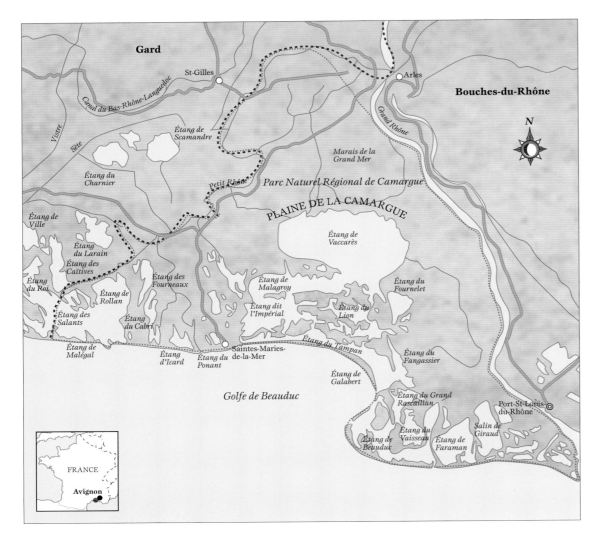

historic private chateaux. This is a trek rich in culture, history and cuisine – a taste of the good life, a ride truly fit for kings and queens.

If the modern French notion of liberty and equality is more your speed, the freedom of an unguided tour in the foothills of the Pyrénées may be of greater appeal to you. This requires a spirit of independence as you set out on your own, guidebook and map in hand, with your horse as your loyal companion. The French call this *randonnée liberté*, a free-range style of touring that they have perfected on their well-marked network of bridle paths and trails called *sentiers de grande randonnée*.

Further south, the warm, golden sun of the Spanish borderlands beckons as does the classic scenery and sensual delights of Provence, a region that has inspired artists, writers and film makers for generations. But most evocative of all – and for me, the quintessential French riding experience – is the Camargue, where a horseback tour is your passport beyond the tourist façade into the fascinating world of the *gardians*, the cowboys who live and work in this underwater wonderland.

La Camargue is the wide, marshy delta of the Rhône River; a spongy, fragile fretwork of sea and silt carried from the Swiss Alps. Large portions of this wetland, which covers 130km^2 (50sq. miles), is designated as a nature reserve; a habitat rich in animal and bird life, including marsh and sea birds, waterfowl, birds of prey and beautiful pink flamingos.

The human history of this sparsely populated environment is one of an incessant struggle against nature, an attempt to contain the salty waters and transform the inhospitable terrain into productive farmland. The land has been cultivated since the Middle Ages, drained, fertilized and protected by low dykes. Over the years, the region has successfully produced rice, grain and even grapes; but by far the biggest industry is the production of salt, with salt pans and

ABOVE LEFT *The two icons of the Camargue, the black bulls and the white horses, graze side by side on the marshy grasslands.*

pyramids adding a strange, somewhat extraterrestrial appearance to the coastal landscape.

This is also cattle territory, the domain of black bulls – the most iconic symbol of the Camargue tradition. These enormous animals with their lyre-shaped horns and fierce demeanour are raised both for meat and the bullring, where they are revered with a passion. These semi-wild beasts roam free in herds, grazing on stretches of land made hard and brittle by salt and the baking sun.

Living alongside the black bulls is the famous white Camargue Horse, a distinctive breed that

ABOVE *Guests have the opportunity to join in cattle ranch activities, including rounding up the semi-wild black bulls.*

was only officially recognized in 1978. It has inhabited these swamplands since time immemorial, long before humans filtered into the region. Some say the bulls and horses migrated together from Asia; others say it's one of Europe's original breeds, a descendant of the horse depicted in prehistoric cave paintings at Lascaux in Southern France.

According to a local legend, the white horse was a gift from Neptune, given to the people of the Camargue to help them manage the terrible black bull that was making their lives difficult. 'This is the best horse I have,' the god told them. 'If you manage to deal with him, he will be a very precious ally against that black bull. Remember, he comes from the sea and was led from a god, so anytime he wants to run back to

the sea, leave him.' Whatever its origins, the Camargue Horse has adapted perfectly to its harsh environment, feeding off salty grasses, water reeds and goosefoot, a tough plant that most other grazing animals cannot digest. Never stabled, it lives permanently outdoors in roaming herds, enduring the incredible heat of summer and the bone-chilling winds that whip off the Alps in the winter months.

Born dark brown or black, the Camargue Horse becomes white with maturity, its light hue a defence against the sun's burning rays and a natural mosquito repellent. It is a small, sturdy, heavily muscled animal, not exactly handsome but surefooted and reliable; a true four-wheel-drive with one leg planted squarely in each corner! These animals have incredible stamina,

ploughing through a metre of mud with ease; yet in the arena, they are nimble and agile with a sharp turn of foot and great acceleration. For the *gardians*, or attendants of the swamps, these horses are indispensable work instruments possessing a natural 'cow-sense' and putting up with no nonsense from the bulls, which tend to be more fractious than most domestic cattle. It is the opportunity to ride these amazing, hard-

working cow ponies under traditional conditions that makes the treks organized by Anna Widstrand from World Horse Riding so appealing. The horses she uses are the personal breeding stock of a local *gardian*, ridden in the traditional Camargue manner – Western style, with long stirrups and reins held in one hand. The saddles are of the local Camargue design, deep-seated and comfortable with caged stirrups to prevent the

foot from slipping through. A visit to a saddlery where these works of art are tooled makes an interesting diversion during the stay in the village.

By virtue of friendship and personal contacts, Anna also has access to private property, leading rides on two large cattle ranches normally closed to tourists. Special permission is also granted to the locals to explore the pine forests and beaches of La Petite Camargue, as well as *l'Étang du*

Fangassier, the lagoon where the flamingos nest. This is visited only out of nesting season.

Setting off from comfortable hotel accommodation close to Les Saintes Maries de la Mer, the first destination is the cattle ranch of Mas des Barnacles where riders may join the local cowboys performing their daily cattle duties, including cutting and calf branding. Later in the week, the focus shifts to Mas de la Belugue, a ranch belonging to one of the Camargue's oldest cattle families. Here, you can ride among herds of Spanish and Camargue bulls, participate in amusing horseback games, and visit herds of Camargue mares and colts grazing in the marshlands. These mares have generally only been handled once – the day they were branded – so they are often distrustful of human presence.

Conducted only during low season when crowds are at a minimum, these treks also feature some great beach riding with 20km (12 miles) of dunes, sand and hard-packed clay flats for the horses to have free rein. There are plenty of opportunities for a canter on this ride, though the tempo can be restricted by ground conditions, particularly if it's muddy!

The Provençal cuisine is rightly famous, a pot pourri of local seafood and shellfish oozing with herbs and garlic; juicy Camargue steaks served with potatoes *au gratin à la Française*; fresh salads and local cheeses; and, of course, the delectable local wines of the region. Lunches are served picnic-style – great slabs of crusty bread stuffed with fresh local produce, the perfect prelude to a doze among long grasses in the warmth of the midday sun.

A highlight for many visitors to the Camargue is the opportunity to attend a bullfight, *course à la cocarde*. Unlike Spanish bullfights, no blood is shed in these tournaments – at least, no bovine blood! The real risk is for the *raseteurs* who attempt to pluck a red pom-pom from between the horns, which is risky as the bulls are stirred into a frenzy by the roaring crowd, the call of the trumpet and the strains of the *Toreador* theme from *Carmen*.

These bulls are extremely aggressive, rebellious, and cunning, hence named the legendary kings of the ring.

These amazing creatures embody the spirit of the Camargue – wild, stirring, passionate. It is an extraordinary world, which, when presented in a genuine manner, offers a compelling riding experience that will have you coming back time after time.

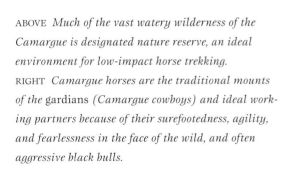

ABOVE *Much of the vast watery wilderness of the Camargue is designated nature reserve, an ideal environment for low-impact horse trekking.*
RIGHT *Camargue horses are the traditional mounts of the* gardians *(Camargue cowboys) and ideal working partners because of their surefootedness, agility, and fearlessness in the face of the wild, and often aggressive black bulls.*

The Forests and Beaches of Andalucia

The Forests and Beaches of Andalucia
ANDALUCIA, SPAIN

Location *Costa de la Luz, southern Spain*

Getting there *Flight to Gibraltar; 90-minute car transfer*

Season *Year round*

Duration *7 nights; 8 days*

Group size *Maximum of 8 riders*

Horses *Andalucian, Andalucian cross, Welsh cob*

Tack *English; helmets advised*

Pace *Moderate*

Riding ability *Intermediate*

'The man who does not love a horse cannot love a woman.' SPANISH PROVERB

The Spanish are not reserved in their praise of the Andalucian Horse. It is revered in literature and poetry as the most beautiful and noble creature in the world, the chosen one of kings and heroes. The horse is essential to Spain's history, the cornerstone of the nation's identity. It embodies the culture, life, and passion; it is the music from their guitars, the wine in their goblets, the sunshine on the hills, the blood spilled in the bullring…

Of ancient and pure ancestry, the Andalucian or *Pura Raza Española* has fought on the battlefields of Europe, found its place in royal courts, and been protected by the church. Its endurance, beauty and athleticism has been praised since the time of the Phoenicians – Homer wrote about it in the Illiad in 1100BC and the famous Greek cavalry officer, Xenophon, waxed lyrical about the 'gifted Iberian horse'.

The Andalucian, which is named after the Spanish region where it was bred and perfected, is a delight to behold – strongly built yet elegant with a thick crested neck, flowing mane and tail, and a short, compact body. Its head is straight and fine with a broad, intelligent forehead, and its large oval eyes are the windows to its gentle soul. Eighty per cent of Andalucians are grey or white, while the rest are bay or black in colour.

During the Roman occupation of Spain this handsome creature was bred as a warhorse – its strength, agility, courage and speed placed it above all others in an era when a man's life literally depended on his mount. Its qualities were also recognized by the Moorish conquerors who crossbred it with their own Arab and Barb horses.

After the Moors were driven out of Spain in the 15th century, the reputation of the Spanish horse spread throughout Europe. It became known as the 'Royal Horse of Europe', esteemed by kings and noblemen; it was also the favoured horse of grand riding academies across the continent, famed for its elegance, impulsion and gymnastic ability.

In 1667 the master horseman, the Duke of Newcastle, wrote of the Andalucian: 'It is the noblest horse in the world, the most beautiful that can be. He is of great spirit and of great courage and docile; hath the proudest trot and the best action in his trot, the loftiest gallop, and is the lovingest and gentlest horse, and fittest of all for a king in his day of triumph.'

No other breed has had such a widespread influence on the development of the modern horse than the Andalucian. From the famed dancing Lipizzaner stallions of the Spanish Riding School to Welsh Mountain ponies, Connemara and German warmbloods; all have their roots in Spanish bloodlines.

ABOVE LEFT *The Andalucian Horse forms part of the romance, tradition and pageantry of the Spanish fiesta.*

OPPOSITE *A headlong gallop along the coastline during low season is a special attraction of riding in southern Spain.*

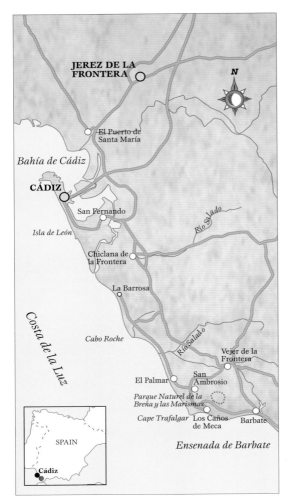

When the conquistadors began their conquest of the New World, the indigenous people of Central America saw them as centaurs; mythical and fearsome creatures that moved as one with their horses. Cortés, conqueror of Mexico, proclaimed 'After God, we owed our victory to the horses.' The Andalucian blood certainly lives on in the modern breeds of the Americas – the American Quarter Horse, Peruvian Paso and Criollo all owe their solid structures, dependability and ostentatious manner to their Spanish heritage.

Centuries of warfare, however, took its toll and by Napoleonic times, the Andalucian breed was threatened with extinction in its homeland. Fortunately, Spanish pride in its national treasure

LEFT *A high-stepping Andalucian Horse, the favoured breed of the royal courts of Europe, performs in the show ring.*

prevailed. Resisting all temptation to interbreed, the purity of the bloodline was ensured by a group of Carthusian monks who bred the horses in monasteries of Seville and Jerez. The purest strain of Andalucian horses owes their survival to the dedication of these superb horse breeders, who considered their animals second only to God.

Today, the historic reverence shown toward these magnificent creatures persists; an inheritance handed down through the generations. The Spanish horse is deified in fiestas, parades, in the

BELOW *Some riding stables offer dressage and show jumping instruction as an adjunct to trail riding in southern Spain.*

show ring and the bullring, and its undeniable beauty and versatility make it one of the most desirable riding horses in the world.

Little wonder, then, that so many equestrians flock to the sunbaked hills of southern Spain to ride these magnificent horses in their natural environment! Spain is one of the most attractive, popular riding destinations in Europe, offering an irresistible combination of warm weather, beautiful beaches, a fascinating culture and, of course, fabulous riding on an equine aristocrat.

While riding tours are available throughout Spain, from the Catalan Pyrenees to the island of Majorca, most commercial treks are based in Andalucia. This is regional Spain at its most

evocative – quaint villages resounding with the passionate strains of flamenco; sun-drenched haciendas surrounded by olive groves and fields of sunflowers; forests of pine and cork oak; and sandy beaches overlooking the northern coastline of Africa. There are also mountain trails through the lofty heights of the Sierra Nevada, offering incredible vistas and endless solitude in a region well off the tourist trail.

This is a multifaceted destination offering a variety of riding experiences in a rich cultural and historic context. As well as excellent trail riding, there is also the appeal of good food, lively evening entertainment and colourful village life. Some tours include visits to wineries, flamenco displays and bullfights; and many offer a visit to

the Royal Andalucian School of Equestrian Art in Jerez, where Andalucian stallions are trained in high school classical dressage.

Taking this one step further is the British Horse Society-approved Epona Riding Centre in Seville, which offers a combination of trail riding and instruction in dressage and jumping from qualified instructors. With excellent facilities and a range of horses trained in every discipline, this is the perfect riding holiday for dedicated equestrians who require more from their vacation experience than just beautiful scenery.

Southern Spain, of course, offers scenery in abundance – no more so than on the beaches of the delightfully named Costa de la Luz, the 'Coast of Light'. Stretching for 200km (124 miles) from the Portuguese border to Gibraltar, this part of Andalucia is an undiscovered gem, unspoiled by tourist development and retaining its Spanish

---

ABOVE *A forest campsite bordering coastal dunes provides a shady resting place for horses and riders on the Costa de la Luz.*

flavour. Dunes, nature reserves and forests back long sandy beaches; and simple fishing villages provide a seafood bonanza of tuna, mussels and prawns. Inland, the cities of Jerez and Cadiz abound in culture and tradition, while white-washed villages lie nestled in floral hillsides offering a timeless slice of rural Spanish life.

This is a region of pure sensory delights – days of endless sunshine and relaxation; exotic food consumed with gusto; the rich palette of Spanish wines and liqueurs; and long nights of song, dance and passion. This is the home of flamenco, the sorrowful and dramatic music of the gypsy community; visit any bar in the region and you're likely to witness performances of this passionate song and dance in its purest, most spontaneous form. This is also the setting for some of the most tempting riding experiences in

providing a luxury holiday experience on well-trained and impeccably turned out horses.

Most of their horses are Andalucians and Andalucian-Arab crosses, but they also have two Welsh cobs imported from England to carry heavier riders. The Andalucian horses were all

True to the relaxed nature of southern Spain, there is a house-party feel at Los Alamos. Accommodation is provided in a large Spanish hacienda set in its own private gardens with citrus trees and a swimming pool, so guests quickly feel like they are staying with friends.

Spain, where the diversity of terrain and the luminosity of the landscape are matched only by the quality of horses.

At Los Alamos – a ranch situated in the small coastal village of Los Canos de Meca – the emphasis is on fun, carefree trekking with plenty of opportunities for fast-paced riding through forest trails, past coastal reserves and along windswept sandy beaches stretching for over 10km (six miles). This British-owned organization, which has only been in business since 2001, is rapidly gaining a reputation for

purchased in the area as four- and five-year-olds, and trained to the highest standards by the owners and their experienced staff. While the horses are well schooled and know the terrain intimately, the holiday is aimed at competent riders who are comfortable at all paces in a range of environments, including open spaces.

ABOVE *The soft sandy trails of the coastal dunes entice riders from all over the world to the Andalucian region of Spain.*

Meals are an important part of the holiday experience, with Mediterranean delicacies prepared by a chef who ran her own restaurant in the UK before settling in Spain. Two days a week, picnics are hosted in the forest while on the other days the ride stops at local taverns that offer a warm welcome, great food, and an insight into the local way of life. With few foreign tourists in the area, the Los Alamos riders are often the only strangers in these bars, inviting a lively cross-cultural exchange. Los Alamos sits on the fringe of the 5000ha (12,355-acre) *Parque*

Naturel de la Breña y Las Marismas, a delightfully pungent forest of pine and eucalyptus scattered with wild sage, rosemary and lavender. The going in the forest makes for fabulous riding, with sandy firebreaks that weave through trees providing the perfect opportunity for a long collected canter.

Even more exhilarating is the chance to let loose on the sandy beaches of Cape Trafalgar and El Palmar, a dream come true for most riders, and a great way for the horses to let off steam. This is the postcard image of Spain – galloping through rolling surf on a fiery Andalucian steed,

ABOVE *Cantering along the tide line at Cape Trafalgar, the perfect adrenaline rush during the winter months.*

water spraying, sand flying, wind in your hair, and a huge grin on your very satisfied face!

It's probably worth noting here that under Spanish law, riding along the tide line is prohibited between the months of June and September (high season), with the horses restricted to the sandy dunes flanking the shore. During the winter months, however, these rules are more relaxed, with the opportunity for fantastic gallops along completely deserted stretches of beach. Wendy A Semel described her experience of the ride: 'Christmas Day was definitely one of the highlights of the trip – we started off with champagne on horseback down at the field, rode off to the beach (with tinsel in horses' bridles and grins on our faces), and we had a blisteringly fast gallop along the tide. But it got even better, because Rachel had a surprise for us on the way home: leading us through a small salt-water lake near the beach, she looked back at us with a wicked gleam in her eye, nodded, and we cantered off three abreast through the lake. When we stopped at the other side, we were doubled over laughing and dripping wet... without a doubt, the best ride I've ever had...'

After this adrenaline-pumping experience, the ride heads back to an ancient Roman road that was built along two impressive cliffs, Torre del Tajo and Los Caños de Meca, which tower over 100m (328ft) above the Atlantic. This is a protected coastal reserve, one of the most unspoiled parts of the coast that provides a safe haven for colonies of herring gulls and egrets nesting in the nooks and crannies. From a Moorish watchtower, El Tajo, there is a spectacular panorama across Cape Trafalgar, with views stretching as far as Africa.

Here, back in 1805, Lord Nelson faced the might of the French fleet; today, the only battles are among windsurfers vying for the best waves. A lighthouse dominates the sandy promontory – an important site since ancient times when a temple dedicated to Juno was used for sacrifices.

The Los Alamos horse trek also takes to the rolling hills of El Campo, riding along ancient drovers' roads and cattle tracks to the little hamlet of San Ambrosia, a slice of medieval Spain with its whitewashed walls and old monasteries.

This is a place resonating with the true spirit of Andalucia – timeless, lyrical, sensual – a place where men of God breed horses, where horsemen are welcome strangers, and a noble Andalucian steed is worth more than riches.

RIGHT *A bareback ride through the surf epitomizes the freedom of a riding holiday along the beaches of southern Spain.*

Bridle Trails of Umbria

ℬridle Trails of Umbria
UMBRIA, ITALY

Location *Assisi*

Getting there *Fly from Rome to Perugia; car or train transfers to Assisi*

Season *March–November*

Duration *6 nights; 4 days of riding*

Group size *Minimum of 2; maximum of 6 riders*

Horses *Quarter Horse, Andalucian crosses*

Tack *English; helmets recommended*

Pace *Moderate*

Riding ability *Intermediate*

*I*TALY IS LIKE A WONDROUS PAINTING, AN IMPRESSIONISTIC canvas with seductive light, rich earthy hues and bold brushstrokes. Few who visit her fail to appreciate the artistry, the perfection. Being there we were more than just observers in a gallery – we became a part of this timeless landscape, participants in its rituals. On the back of our shiny steeds, we rode into history; we were the hills cloaked in morning mist, the olive groves, the fields of sunflowers bathed in golden sunshine; the song, wine, and passion.

For those who love the good things in life, Italy is a veritable feast for the senses, a place for hungry eyes, minds, souls and stomachs. It is a place where indulgence is acceptable, and the ultimate hedonism – horse riding – seems only natural and the perfect way to savour its delights. *La Dolce Vita* indeed!

It is the gentle hills and villages of the northern regions of Tuscany and Umbria – areas offering delightful scenery and rich traditions – that most appeal to equestrians. While good, fit horses and well-planned treks are prerequisites, it is the attention to detail that makes these rides so special – the first-class accommodation, warmth and hospitality of the Italian people, great food and wine, and the all-pervading history of the region.

Despite its rural ambience and traditions such as the Palio horse race held annually in Siena, horse-based vacations are not common in Italy, unlike in neighbouring France or Spain. Farms that do offer extended treks into the countryside tend to be represented by overseas agents, rather than local tourist authorities; so it's essential to plan your vacation well in advance.

While most American and British tourists gravitate toward the well-publicized delights of Tuscany with its dreamy landscape of rolling hills, vineyards, olive groves and ancient hilltop villages, the neighbouring region of Umbria, known as the 'Green Heart of Italy', offers all the charm and beauty of Tuscany without the crowds. This is a part of Italy brimming with history, blessed with a sweet, gentle pace and a timeless ambience – a place to rest, contemplate and absorb the nuances of Italian life.

Here, walled medieval towns cling tenaciously to mountain tops and rambling farmhouses nestle in scalloped valleys lined with cypress pines and olive groves, the fields ablaze with sunflowers. Ancient Roman roads crisscross the countryside, while crumbling terracotta ruins reveal the secrets of the mysterious Etruscans who were the original inhabitants of this land. It is a quiet and peaceful scenario; a place infused with the spirit of St Francis of Assisi, the patron saint of animals.

Born in Assisi in 1182, St Francis lived a life of privilege before a series of traumatic events caused him to turn his back on worldly riches, embracing a simple lifestyle based on the pure ideals of the Gospels. He lived as a hermit in the hills of Assisi, communing with nature and helping the poor; he attracted followers who were drawn to his sincerity, piety, and joy. After his death in 1228, a basilica was erected in his honour in the town of Assisi – not exactly in

ABOVE LEFT *Fine horses and an artistic sensibility steeped in history are an irresistible combination on a horse trek in Italy.*

OPPOSITE *Two riders gently guide their horses through a shallow riverbed.*

keeping with his humble philosophy, but a magnificent monument, nevertheless, to one of the world's most revered religious figures.

Today, Assisi is the most prominent city in Umbria. It is a major pilgrimage site and a magnet for tourists who flock to its beautiful rose-coloured churches and piazzas. Closed to vehicle traffic, the best way to explore its cobbled lanes and hidden passages is on foot, taking time to shop in its boutiques and craft stores, rest in its outdoor cafes, and soak up its medieval atmosphere. Although devastated by a major earthquake in 1997, much of the restoration work is now complete. The Basilica of San Francesco with its priceless frescoes is once again open for public admiration.

Just a few kilometres from Assisi, nestled at the foot of Mt Subasio among oak and olive trees is Malvarina Country Inn, a 15th-century working farm that also operates as a bed-and-breakfast establishment. This lovely estate is part of a government programme called *Agritourismo* – to qualify for this programme, there must be less than 30 beds available, and the property must bring in more profit from agriculture than tourism. Malvarina produces its own delicious honey, bread, jam, salami and olive oil – all of which find their way onto the menu of a restaurant reserved for guests.

Malvarina is surrounded by gorgeous countryside, conveniently located, and incredibly picturesque. Small and intimate, it provides a unique opportunity to experience rural Italian life at its finest, and to interact with the host family who openly welcomes guests into their daily routine.

The inn is run by the Fabrizi family – the gregarious Claudio, his wife Patrizia and their sons Filippo and Giacomo. The matriarch of the clan is Maria Maurillo, universally known as Mamma. Now in her seventies, Mamma is a gourmet chef, lauded internationally as a true master of authentic regional Umbrian cooking. When she's not preparing delicious meals from local

ABOVE RIGHT *Riders with a passion for history and culture will delight in stopping over at atmospheric ruins such as these.*

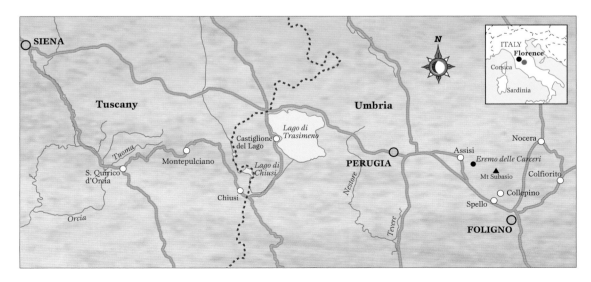

farm produce for the appreciative guests, this energetic woman runs cooking classes, sharing the secrets of real Italian cooking with small groups of chefs.

The world-class meals, warm Italian hospitality and atmospheric lodgings in beautiful surrounds are very enticing. A brisk ride on one of Claudio's magnificent horses will definitely leave you with a desire to come back for more. Claudio himself is an excellent horseman, and his stable of fit and shiny Quarter Horse/Andalucian crosses are forward going and responsive. The tall, leggy and impeccably groomed horses are ridden in English tack, which is also exquisitely cared for.

There are two weekly Malvarina riding packages available; one ride is based at Malvarina, the other a progressive trip delightfully called *I Sentieri del Tempo* – The Paths of Time. This trek goes from Assisi to Colfiorito – a plateau in the middle of the Apennines – to

ABOVE *A beautifully preserved building provides a superb backdrop for a photo opportunity in the Italian countryside.*

Nocera, an ancient town famous for its natural springs and mineral water. Every night the riders stay in different places, savouring many local dishes and tasting the local specialties of wine and olive oil along the way.

The Malvarina package consists of four full days in the saddle, with one day off to explore Umbria at a more modern pace. Every day you ride out from the farmhouse in a different direction, past the Malvarina fountain through olive groves and along roads and bridle paths dating back to Roman times, thus following in the footsteps of saints of old. Picture-book villages,

remote churches and ancient burial sites are all part of the itinerary, with lively trots down cobbled streets followed by carefree canters through fields strewn with wildflowers adding to the experience.

Of course, Mamma Maria's wonderful cooking is always within reach, with a simple picnic lunch showcasing the best of the local produce.

Di Smith was also impressed with Mamma's cooking. He explained, 'We reached the grove on horseback after crossing a stony stream through fields of crimson poppies to find that long table already set with Mamma's delicious pesto and red tomatoes and olives and bread and wine (of course). Ho hum. Life at Malvarina. To see Assisi from horseback winding down those cobbled streets is a rare experience. It remains in my memory as everything that embodies Umbria. The scenery, the house and the home-cooked food. I also remember the horses stabled there as being particularly happy and fit, which is a joy to behold. Perhaps if I lived there permanently my coat would shine too!'

While you cannot actually take the horses beyond the walls into Assisi, the first day's ride explores the outskirts of the city, clattering through the cobbled streets in the shadow of medieval and Renaissance buildings. This ride culminates in a visit to Rocca Maggiore, a fortified castle strategically positioned on a rock promontory overlooking the town, a vestige of more turbulent times.

A more peaceful destination is the silent beauty of Eremo delle Carceri, a remote hermitage hidden in a deep gorge on the slopes of Mt Subasio. This is where St Francis and his followers retired to pray and fast; the tiny grotto favoured by the saint is still used today as a place of solitary meditation. Riders dismount and walk up to this holy place, enjoying magnificent valley views along the way.

Every village presents a ride through time, a journey through the pages of Italy's fascinating

LEFT *Italy is the ideal riding environment for those who want to experience its history, art and culture.*

past. In the picturesque hilltop town of Colle-pino, the beautifully restored medieval castle stands as a silent Sentinel; its thick walls and five defence towers were impenetrable barriers throughout the ages. Another lovely town is Spello, city of 100 churches and home to famous frescoes by the Renaissance master Pintur-icchio, which can be seen in the Church of Santa Maria Maggiore.

The final day's riding takes you through fields of wild porcini mushrooms to the peak of the turtle-shaped Mt Subasio, where riders are treated to a spectacular 360-degree pano-rama of the Umbrian countryside. From this elevation, one can appreciate the scale and harmony of this very human landscape with its patchwork of villages and rural hamlets dotted among the rolling hills.

As evening descends upon Malvarina, the activity centres on the converted wine cellar where Mamma Maria prepares the evening feast for the hungry riders. She serves a cornu-copia of local delicacies – truffles sniffed from

ABOVE *Horseback riding through medieval villages is a unique way of getting close to Italian history and culture.*

the earth by sharp-nosed dogs, ripe tomatoes plucked straight from the vine, olives crushed in the farm's own vats. With an open fire roar-ing and the long, communal tables prepared for multiple courses, the mood is set for an evening of feasting and stimulating conversation, bot-tles of Umbrian wine a welcome accompani-ment to the parade of gourmet delights – the perfect end to a long day.

It is all part of an unforgettable experience, a horseback adventure into a world where the magnificent scenery is matched only by the gracious hospitality and incredible warmth of the Italian people.

Csikós of the Puszta

Csikós of the Puszta
SOMOGY REGION, HUNGARY

Location *Keleviz, Somogy*

Getting there *Train, car or bus from Budapest*

Season *May–August*

Duration *7 nights; 8 days*

Group size *Maximum of 10 riders*

Horses *Hungarian Kisber, Arab & Lipizzaner crosses*

Tack *English; helmets advised*

Pace *Varied*

Riding ability *Intermediate*

HORSES ARE TO HUNGARY WHAT PAPRIKA IS TO goulash – the essential ingredient, the spice of life, the fire in the veins! Ever since the fearsome Magyar warriors swept across the Verecke Pass into the vast steppes of Hungary over 1000 years ago, the horse has been a friend, partner, and ally in peace and war. It has helped to shape the nation; in return, it has been loved, protected and revered as a national icon. Hungary is what it is largely because of the horse, and it seems this alliance has a very strong future as the rest of the world rediscovers its hidden treasures.

The Magyars were the greatest equestrian nation of their time, remarkably skilled horsemen who rode their swift horses backwards at a gallop, firing arrows and wielding sabres, lances and axes. After occupying the Carpathian Basin in AD896, they raided far and wide, striking fear in the hearts of Christian Europe for more than half a century. In the monasteries of Rome, Greece and Spain, the fervent prayer could be heard: 'From the arrows of the Hungarians, deliver us, O Lord!'

The Magyars reign of terror ended in AD955 when they suffered a disastrous defeat at the hands of the Germans. In disarray, the tribes gave up their nomadic ways and adopted Christianity, forming an alliance with the Holy Roman Empire. In the year 1000, the Magyar prince Stephen was crowned King; and the nation of Hungary was officially born.

The legacy of the warrior horsemen, however, endured – Hungary's cavalry went from strength to strength, evolving into the legendary Hussars of the 18th and 19th centuries. Horse breeding also thrived, the Hungarian horses protected with export bans and customs tariffs until well into the Middle Ages. Horse-drawn carriages – the first in the world – were invented; the word 'coach' is said to have derived from the town of Kocs, famed for its cart and wagon builders. The Hungarians were also the first to develop harnesses, trappings and various driving methods – pairs, teams and five-in-hand – an incredible contribution not only to the equestrian world, but also to modern life in general.

Arguably the most visible vestige of the Magyar tradition, however, is found on the *puszta* – the Great Plains of Hungary. This flat expanse, which occupies over a third of Hungary's entire area, is home to the *csikós*, the traditional Hungarian horse herders whose unique style of horsemanship has come to embody the Hungarian spirit. The *csikós* is to the *puszta* what the American cowboy is to the Wild West – a symbol of freedom, romance and independence.

Like the Magyars of old, the *csikós* are impressive riders, galloping herds of loose horses across the plains, whips cracking, voices hollering, their culotte-like riding trousers flapping in the wind. Traditionally, they ride on girthless leather pads; in some areas, they even straddle bareback. While their skills are genuine, many of them have made their mark at tourist shows and rodeos, performing riding,

ABOVE LEFT *The traditional equestrian skills of the Magyar horsemen are embodied in the contemporary* csikós *culture of Hungary.*

OPPOSITE *Wearing traditional riding culottes and wielding a whip, a Hungarian* csikós *gallops across the* Puszta, *the Great Plains of Hungary.*

knife and whip tricks (including the manly art of 'wife beating'!) to many appreciative audiences. The most famous trick of all is the Puszta-Five, also known as the Koch-Five after the Austrian artist who dreamed up this amazing feat 100 years before it was actually performed. It is a supreme test of horsemanship; five horses gallop in formation – three at the front, two at the back – mastered by a *csikós* standing on the backs of the last two horses. This is a test of balance and control, and it also helps to be a little crazy, a dedicated and fearless equestrian in the true Magyar tradition.

A *csikós'* performance at a *csarda*, or horse farm, is as much a part of a visit to Hungary as watching a rodeo in the United States. It is pure showmanship performed by genuine working cowboys. The shows are usually followed by a traditional Hungarian goulash meal accompanied by wine, gypsy music, dancing and a carriage tour.

Buoyed by the interest in Hungarian horsemanship, some stables have now extended their programmes and are offering horse treks through the unspoiled Hungarian countryside, reviving the traditions of old and giving visitors the opportunity to experience its superlative

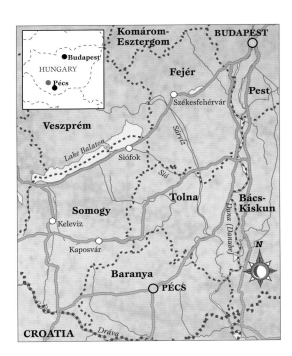

RIGHT *Riders on a Hungarian trek are often accompanied by a* hinto, *a traditional carriage drawn by two horses.*

BELOW *The Hungarian Warmblood is one of the world's most prized saddle horses, displaying physical similarities to its Oriental ancestor, the Turkomen.*

OPPOSITE BOTTOM *The close bond between man and beast is illustrated in the equestrian skills of the* csikós, *the cowboys of the Hungarian plains.*

sporting of the Hungarian Warmbloods. Few countries in the world, however, have experienced political turmoil as frequently as Hungary – and just as war created the Hungarian horse, so it nearly destroyed it. During World War II, more than half of Hungary's finest breeding stock were taken as spoils of war; many others were slaughtered by soldiers for meat or simply killed in battle. Some were given a reprieve – 150 Kisbers were imported to the USA for the US Remount; but when the Remount was disbanded in 1947, the horses were sold at public auction and scattered into oblivion. Only a handful of people appreciated the value of these 'Heavenly Horses', and today there are less than 2000 Kisber Felvers in the world.

In the past 10 years, however, Hungary has undergone somewhat of a renaissance in the traditional pursuits of horse breeding and riding. Leading the revival of equestrian tourism are two passionate horse-lovers, Katalin Almasy and Jozsef Hunyady of Somogy Riding Tours. They are based 180km (112 miles) from Budapest in Hungary's 'green belt', which stretches south of Lake Balaton along the Drava River to the Croatian border.

horse culture first hand. Riders can emulate the *csikós* and their Magyar forebears on the *puszta*; or receive royal treatment in the grounds of castles and grand estates. It is an opportunity to discover a delightful and little known part of Europe – a place that retains the charm, grace and tranquillity of the golden age of horses.

The Hungarian Horse, as we know it today, is the descendent of the Magyar steppe horses – lithe and graceful creatures of Asian and Turkomen bloodlines. Over the generations, interbreeding with Arab and Spanish horses created an athletic, strong and attractive animal; a horse revered as one of the finest in all of Europe. By the 19th century, a leading Thoroughbred stud had developed a half-bred horse called the Kisber Felver – a breed that is today considered the most beautiful and

Katalin and Jozsef's story encapsulates all the romance of Central Europe. Both are from wealthy aristocratic families – the Hunyadys were Counts of the Holy Roman Empire who owned large horse-breeding and wine-producing estates; the Almasys were also famous land-owners and equestrians. Shattered and divided by World War II, both families escaped Hungary to settle in the West; but in the mid-1990s, Katalin and Jozsef returned to the land of their ancestors intent on rediscovering their heritage.

With compensation bonds, Jozsef managed to reclaim family property in Somogy County; and the couple began renovating the estate and embracing the traditions of horse breeding.

The Somogy area is wonderful horse country; peaceful, green and unspoiled. It includes some

BELOW *There is no better way to experience the romance of Hungary, than a bareback ride on a magnificent steed.*

of Europe's wildest and most undiscovered natural areas, a corridor that somehow has escaped industrialization and retains a gentle ambience of bygone days. It is rich in watercourses, ponds and forests teeming with wildlife – including red deer, wild boar, otters and rare birds such as the white-tailed fish eagle and the black and white stork.

The region comes under the management of SPANC, the Somogy County Provincial Association for Nature Conservation, which is an

international nonprofit organization that aims to protect the region's delicate ecosystem.

Enthusiastic environmentalists themselves, Jozsef and Katalin have developed a riding tour in conjunction with SPANC to promote the area to international equestrians. The ride begins at their manor house just outside the village of Keleviz, a lovely bed-and-breakfast establishment set in 4ha (10 acres) of paddocks and parkland with century-old trees. In this picturesque setting guests meet with the staff

of SPANC, to learn about the area through which they'll be riding, and then set off through the open rolling countryside free of paved roads and motor traffic.

In true Hungarian fashion, the horses used on the ride are all exceptional – mostly of

BELOW *Daring balancing acts are a feature of* csikós *showmanship, a popular drawcard for visiting tourists.*

Kisber bloodline, with Arab and Lipizzaner crosses. Most of them belong to Jozsef and Katalin – the others are the property of SPANC. For guests who are not up for six hours a day in the saddle, there is also the option of following the group in a *hinto* – a carriage drawn by two horses. Even experienced but slightly unfit riders will find a rest in the cart beneficial; there are always plenty of helpers who will ride in their place. After two nights of luxury at Jozsef and Katalin's lovely

home, the standard of accommodation becomes a little more basic in Association-owned fishermen's huts along the riverbank – just a step above camping, really, but enhanced by a welcoming campfire and a hearty Hungarian meal. Local specialties, wine and lunchtime picnics all add to the experience, and English guests will be impressed by the endless cups of tea on offer!

Riding through this beautiful region is a little like entering the pages of a fairytale. Quaint villages barely touched by the 21st century; ancient forests, deep and dark, the realm of wild deer and pigs; and chains of lakes, jumping with pike, carp and catfish. The itinerary is a delightful mix of cultural and natural experiences. Lunch breaks are taken in the forests or in typical Hungarian cellars; and on some evenings, riders are given the chance to soak away aches and pains in a famous Hungarian thermal bath – a true Hungarian experience not to be missed.

The focus of this ride, however, is nature – in fact, all profits from the ride go towards the Conservancy fund. Each day, the trek visits a different reserve where nature give an insight into the workings of the ecosystem. For instance, in the lovely wetlands of Petesmalom, the group stops for a close-up view of the famous 'fishponds', a series of lakes that are home to several families of wild otter, as well as rare white-tailed eagle and the ferruginous duck. Here, volunteers are working to improve nesting sites of wildfowl on a lake island.

It is refreshing to discover that, in a country with such a long, complex and often turbulent history, the preservation of nature is still of paramount importance. Thanks to horse-lovers like Katalin and Jozsef, the revival of age-old cultural traditions and equestrian pursuits is having a positive impact on the environment, ensuring that this special part of Central Europe is preserved for future generations of riders.

LEFT *The cool green countryside of Somogy provides a gorgeous backdrop to a trek run in association with SPANC, an international nature organization.*

ABOVE *The rural ambience of Somogy County, with traditional farmhouses, manicured gardens and quiet country lanes adjoining wild corridors of nature.*

Land of Beautiful Horses

Land of Beautiful Horses

CAPPADOCIA, CENTRAL TURKEY

Location *Avanos, Cappadocia*

Getting there *Flight from Istanbul to Nevsehir
or Kayseri; transfer by minibus to Avanos*

Season *April–October*

Duration *7–12 days*

Group size *Minimum 2; maximum of 12*

Horses *Akhal-Teke, Arab, Turkish
mixed-breed*

Tack *English; helmets recommended*

Pace *Moderate*

Riding ability *Intermediate*

THERE IS A NEW CAVALRY CONQUERING THE WORLD, emulating the great horsemen of old, the Alexanders and the Genghis Khans in their thirst for new lands and different cultures. Less ruthless but no less driven, this mounted army's quest is to learn and be enriched. We urge our four-legged steeds to lead us to new experiences, to carry us to the most beautiful places on earth, from sun-kissed golden beaches to lofty mountain heights. From the back of the horse, this planet is ours to explore. And so is Cappadocia.

This is a landscape from another world; a surreal 'Dali-esque' fantasy of twisted cones, pockmarked cliffs and phallic towers sculpted into bizarre formations by a crazed Mother Nature on an artistic frenzy of creation. This suspended reality is Cappadocia, the Land of Beautiful Horses, an alien moonscape of pink and ochre where it seems incongruous to find a human being, let alone a horse. Yet horses are a part of this world, its very heart and soul and there is no better means to discover its mysteries.

The living history museum of Cappadocia has cast its web of intrigue for centuries. Located at the crossroads of Asia and Europe in Central Turkey, Cappadocia has long been a centre of trade, war, worship and refuge. Today, it is Turkey's most visited destination, and considered one of the wonders of the world.

Its amazing story is one of collusion between man and nature, beginning over three million years ago with the violent eruption of two nearby volcanoes, Mt Erciyes and Mt Hasan. Layers of volcanic ash spewed across the region, hardening into a porous rock called *tufa* that was covered, in turn, by a hard layer of basalt lava. Over the millennia, the basalt cracked and split leaving the softer rock vulnerable to the eroding forces of wind, ice and water. The result is the bizarre, barren landscape of canyons, cliffs and huge phallic columns which the Turks naively call 'Fairy Chimneys', perhaps to deflect from more obvious lewd metaphors.

Adjoining this arid wasteland are fertile, sheltered valleys which were settled as early as Neolithic times. Around 1900BC, the land became home to the Hittites, a Persian race who were the contemporaries of the Ancient Egyptians. A people famed for their horse-breeding skills, they named the area Katpatuka, or 'Land of the Beautiful Horses'.

Under constant threat from invading aggressors, the Hittites soon discovered the advantages of living underground; digging into the soft rock to form caves, hand-carved dwellings and even whole subterranean cities. Following this example, the early Christians also fled to Cappadocia seeking refuge from religious persecution, building not only homes in the cliffs, but thousands of churches and rough-hewn monasteries which they decorated with simple frescoes.

During the seventh century, Cappadocia became a bulwark against the Arab invasion, its Christian troglodytes digging deeper and deeper into the rock. From the outside, the cliffs and rocks appeared uninhabited; inside, they hid multistorey cities capable of housing up to 6000 people. Excavations have revealed more than 35

ABOVE LEFT *The title 'Land of Beautiful Horses' is still relevant today in Cappadocia, with locally bred Akhal-Teke horses enhancing the landscape.*

OPPOSITE *A dry, dusty moonscape with 'fairy chimneys' provides a fascinating riding terrain for a group of trekkers in Cappadocia.*

such cities in the Cappadocia region, featuring cramped living quarters, stables for those 'beautiful horses', chapels, schools, complex ventilation systems and communal kitchens still blackened by smoke. Were invaders to discover the entry to these underground villages, huge stones were simply rolled across to block the passageways.

After the establishment of the Ottoman empire, the underground caves were used as mosques, tombs and protective accommodation for traders who travelled the Silk Road. Some of the more elaborate caves were converted into hotels, which are still popular today, while a handful

are still used as private homes complete with satellite dishes. It is the opportunity to explore these mysterious underground cities and churches that attract so many tourists to this fascinating region. Few places in the world are as rich in culture, history and geography; it is also blessed with perfect weather, good food, an extraordinary culture and fabulous shopping, making it an irresistible holiday package.

For equestrians, there is an added bonus: Cappadocia offers great riding opportunities, a chance to explore the land in the manner of its original inhabitants on the back of beautiful

horses. The magnificent steeds in question are the trail horses from the Akhal-Teke Horse Riding Centre, an establishment highly regarded for the quality of its horses and services. As the name suggests, many of these horses are full-blood Akhal-Tekes – classic Oriental horses originating in the deserts of nearby Turkmenistan. This is probably the original breed of horse

---

ABOVE *Elaborate caves carved into the hillside provided refuge for whole communities over centuries; they make an interesting pit stop.*

brought to Cappadocia by the Hittites. It is a legendary creature famed for its speed, grace and golden metallic coat. The Akhal-Teke is the most distinctive and famous strain of the Turkoman – horses prized by great leaders such as Darius and Alexander the Great, and referred to as 'heavenly horses' by invading Chinese armies.

Lithe and streamlined, these forward-going and fast horses are the greyhounds of the equine kingdom. The Akhal-Teke is a true desert breed with a distinctive appearance – a long, often thin neck, strong sloping shoulders, prominent withers and a lean, sinewy body built for speed. Its skin is very thin, with a short, fine and silky coat. A characteristic feature is its short, sparse mane and forelock and scanty tail. In many ways, this horse breaks all the rules of conformation, but the overall impression is of an aristocratic, proud and noble creature with an elegant, refined bearing.

Joining these four-legged supermodels at the Akhal-Teke Riding Centre are a herd of Arab and mixed-breed mares, providing a range of mounts for riders of all abilities. While beginners are welcome on the day rides, guests joining the multi-day treks should have previous trail-riding experience and be prepared to spend up to six hours a day in the saddle. English riding clothing is recommended and hard hats, while not mandatory, are advisable in such rugged terrain.

Camping trips are offered, but many guests at Akhal-Teke choose to stay at comfortable local hotels, indulging in a soft bed, good meals and local entertainment after a long day in the saddle. While the rides explore one of the most amazing landscapes on earth, they are more of a cultural experience than a wilderness trek, affording guests an opportunity to soak up the rich Turkish experience and a unique way of life.

Owner and trek leader Ercihan Dilari is a highly experienced horseman who knows the maze-like trails in the Cappadocian hills like the back of his hand. Fluent in English, French and Turkish, he is an affable and effusive host, his story-telling ability bringing the age-old traditions of the region back to life. 'Each day brought us to a new valley, and every day I declared a

ABOVE *Turkey presents a perfect blend of history and culture for visiting tourists.*

new favourite. Along the trails, Ercihan stopped frequently, often not bothering to dismount, to pick fresh fruit and vegetables from the farmers' fields. He shared grapes and apricots, tomatoes and peppers, mulberries and melons. A rider who doesn't see much value in the trot gait, Ercihan led us at a peaceful walk and invigorating gallops, but gladly acquiesced when requested some healthy, collected canters..' said Karen Stahl.

Setting out from home base at Avanos, the rides feature a different historic location every day, giving guests a much broader perspective of the region than most visiting tourists experience. Avanos itself is a fascinating town, situated on the banks of the river, Kizilirmak, or the Red River. Many artisans live here creating pottery made from the clay deposits that give the river its characteristic red tinge. There is also a weaving school in the town, teaching apprentices the art of dyeing and making traditional carpets and kilims.

These ancient crafts, skills that have been passed down through the generations, are a reminder that Cappadocia is indeed a living museum, a timeless capsule that remains largely unaffected by the

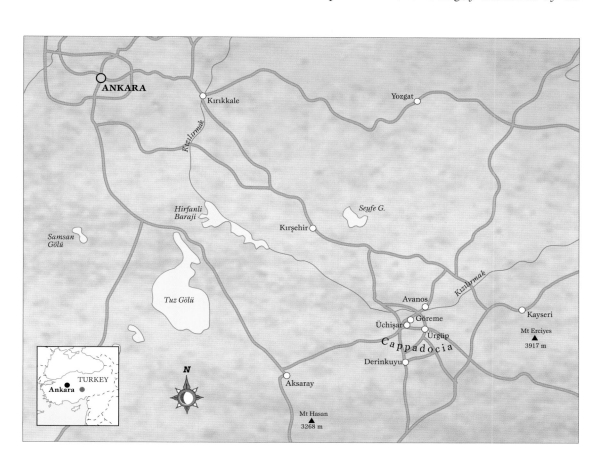

onslaught of the modern world. Every day, the Akhal-Teke trek reveals new wonders, with riders dismounting to admire a romantic 13th-century inn or to explore underground cities. Walking through the dank, dark passageways carved into the hills is an eerie and eye-opening experience, emphasizing just how vulnerable its original inhabitants must have felt. It's a little like entering an underground ant-farm – the walls are close and the ceilings low, inviting claustrophobia. Only the very bravest of armies would have dared attack such a complex and well-defended fortress.

The mind-boggling Pasabag Vadi, or the Valley of Fairy Chimneys, both intrigues and amuses; inevitable ribald comments relating to male genitalia reducing most groups to peals of laughter. Trails crisscross through this valley, so you can wander unrestrained among the bizarre alien forms. Film aficionados may recognize this landscape – it was, in fact, the location for the desert scenes in the original *Star Wars*.

Sunset is the optimum time to visit the Fairy Chimneys because the shadows and afternoon light intensifies the palette of creams, pinks and golds. To silently watch the sky turn to orange behind these truly bizarre formations is a genuinely, unapologetically clichéd 'magical moment'!

The highlight for most visitors to Cappadocia is the Göreme Open Air Museum, which provides a welcome afternoon break from the saddle. This national monument was one of the most important centres for the early Christians who took refuge in its hills and caves between the sixth and 12th centuries. Many of the churches and passageways dug into the cliffs are open for inspection, including Tokali Kilise, or the Church of the Buckle, which is the largest and most important church in the town. At one time, this church housed a collection of gold and precious jewels, including a large gold buckle (hence the name) which mysteriously disappeared.

This site has become somewhat of a place of pilgrimage for Christians but its appeal goes beyond its religious context. The sheer artistry of the town, as well as its historical significance is overwhelming, and few who visit fail to be

moved. It's an amazing testament to man's ability to live in context with the landscape – he has managed to manipulate the environment while living in complete harmony with nature.

About 12km (seven miles) from Göreme is the village of Uçhisar, built around a pinnacle of rock called the Citadel. The view from the castle cut into the *tufa* is simply amazing, described as resembling 'an enormous white sponge or a stone forest'. Once again, nature has been fully exploited here with pigeon holes carved into cliff faces to promote the collection of guano, a vital source of fertilizer in this desert environment.

Despite the wealth of history and amazing scenery, one of the more tangible highlights of the rides through Cappadocia is the effusive Turkish hospitality. In every village, there is an obligatory 'tea stop', with riders dismounting to consume cups of strong tea sweetened with spoonsful of sugar. This tradition will occur not just at cafés, but also at carpet shops and pottery factories, where the simple act of purchasing can become a lengthy and intense performance as the shopkeeper seduces you with his sweet brew!

From the lofty village of Ürgüp, the final day of the seven-day 'Cappadocia Highlight' tour concludes with an invigorating ride through the Red and Rose Valleys, where the light bounces off the cliff faces in stunning shades of pink and russet. From there, it's back to the stables at Avanos for a well-earned celebration and some last-minute shopping in the numerous craft stalls.

Horses and shopping don't often go hand in hand; this is one of the few occasions when a riding holiday results in a suitcase full of souvenirs. This dichotomy, however, is what gives this ride a unique flavour – the cultural and historic elements as essential as the amazing, surreal landscape in this accurately named, 'Land of Beautiful Horses'.

RIGHT *The ever-changing panorama of Cappadocia. Deep crevices cast intriguing shadows as the sun sets over the hills of Avanos.*

Africa

Waterberg Wilderness Adventure

Waterberg Wilderness Adventure

LIMPOPO PROVINCE, SOUTH AFRICA

Location *The Waterberg Mountains*

Getting there *A three-hour drive from Johannesburg International Airport*

Season *Year round*

Duration *Varied; flexible itinerary*

Group size *Equus – maximum of 6 riders; Horizon – maximum of 8 riders*

Horses *Boerperd, Arab, Friesian*

Tack *South African, McClellan saddles*

Pace *Moderate*

Riding ability *Novice to advanced*

In South Africa they call it a 'monkey's wedding' – the magical moment when the sun shines through falling rain. No-one seems to know why it's called that, but when I turned in the saddle to gaze upon this glorious phenomenon, it felt like I was witnessing a sacred event, the conjugal union of Mother Nature with her lover, Africa. A shard of afternoon sunlight had pierced the angry storm clouds, bathing the verdant pasture and its dramatic escarpment backdrop in a warm golden glow. A vapour mist was softly falling, glistening on grassy husks like diamonds twinkling in the breeze, while across the inky sky, a double rainbow formed two perfect arches, a colourful decree announcing the passing of the storm.

The pioneer conservationist Clive Walker once commented, 'The Waterberg is like an indelible ink – once experienced, never to be erased.' There are few moments of pure perfection etched in my memory, but that stormy afternoon ride in the northern wilderness of South Africa is a permanent vision. At that moment, I believed I had found my paradise. There is no better combination, in my mind, than magnificent scenery, good company and kind, willing horses. Add to that amazing wildlife and you'll begin to understand why South Africa is one of the premier riding destinations in the world.

For visitors venturing into the 'Dark Continent' for the first time, South Africa is a great place to start; it is well serviced, politically stable and easily accessible. For most tourists it is also comparatively cheap with a favourable exchange rate against most major currencies. Despite its relative urbanization, the country's main attractions lie beyond its cities – amazing scenery, world-class national parks and of course the animal life of the African plains.

For horseback riders, South Africa offers some wonderful equestrian opportunities encapsulating the 'Out of Africa' experience. You can explore the wine trails of the Western Cape, trek the rugged passes of the Drakensberg Range, or ride the battlefields near Durban for an added historical dimension.

For a fascinating cultural experience, pony trekking in the inland kingdom of Lesotho – the Kingdom in the Sky – provides a genuine insight into a traditional way of life. The Basotho are renowned as a nation of horsemen, and for generations the surefooted Basotho pony has been used as transport in the rugged mountains. On these eco-treks, villagers provide the horses, guides and hut accommodation – your riding experience, therefore contributes to the local economy.

In the remote northern province of Limpopo, the Waterberg Mountains offer breathtaking panoramas of vast African plains stretching for miles across a boundless horizon. This rugged range runs for 150km (93 miles) east to west, covering around 14,500km (9010 miles). The name *Thaba Meetse*, in the local Sotho language, means 'mountains of water', referring to the diversity of habitats found in the area.

PREVIOUS PAGES *A local Ndebele woman admires a horse in the Greater Waterberg region.*
ABOVE LEFT *The Boerperd, descendent of the Cape Horse, makes a reliable companion in the ruggedly beautiful Waterberg wilderness region.*
OPPOSITE *Take a moment to admire the amazing palette of the South African bush as the evening sun filters through the leaves.*

Here, space takes on new meaning – the open vistas overwhelm, liberate, and inspire. This land, once eschewed as a hostile place of exile for troublesome politicians, is today a veritable horsy heaven offering some of the best riding in the Southern Hemisphere. Several highly regarded horse-riding establishments are based in this part of the world, and it has become a magnet for adventure-loving tourists from all over.

One of the main attractions for overseas visitors is, of course, the opportunity to ride amongst wild game. South Africa is ranked as the third most biologically diverse country in the world. Here, the challenge is how to protect the environment while coping with the demands and needs of over 40 million citizens. Only six per cent of South Africa is under formal protection, but an ever-increasing amount of land is being reclaimed as farmers recognize the commercial potential of stocking their properties with game.

Outside the major national parks, much of South Africa's game viewing is restricted to the private game reserves where the presence of fences is a niggling reminder of human domination over nature. The animals might be indigenous and the habitats genuine, but there is never that overwhelming sense of freedom and scale that you experience in true wilderness such as Botswana's Okavango Delta. You could call it a civilized view of the landscape, which may or may not appeal to visiting tourists, depending on their expectations.

ABOVE *Swimming among water lilies in Horizon's dam is a unique way for the mounts to cool down after a long ride.*

OPPOSITE *Riders pick up the pace as they venture through a dry creek bed – the smiles on their faces say it all!*

For the guests at Horizon Horseback Adventures, game viewing within a fenced enclosure cannot diminish the excitement of coming within metres of some of the most majestic creatures in the world. A horseback safari offers unparalleled game viewing; not only is it quieter and more intimate than a jeep safari, but the wild plains' animals don't seem to be afraid of the horse, accepting it as just another herd creature. Riders will be overwhelmed by the sight of a gangly giraffe bending in an awkward attempt to drink from a waterhole, or the flash of black and white as a zebra darts through scrub; these experiences are enriched by the sensual liberation of horse riding.

At Horizon, the emphasis is on horses and horsemanship. Many of its herds of honest Boerperd, Anglo-Arab and Thoroughbred have

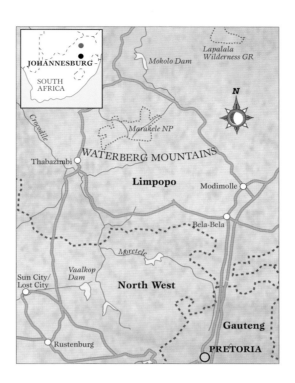

been reared, broken and schooled by Shane Dowinton using natural 'round-pen reasoning' techniques. He runs Horizon with his English-born wife, Laura. As well as the daily game safaris, guests are also encouraged to participate in other equestrian disciplines such as cross-country jumping, Western games and polocrosse – fun activities that give this horse riding holiday an extra dimension.

Horizon is based on the Triple B Ranch, one of the oldest family farms in the Waterberg Mountains. This working cattle ranch and crop farm offers 8299ha (20,000 acres) of flat riding country, including a private game reserve and a myriad of trails surrounding a beautiful hippopotamus-filled dam which provides a spectacular backdrop for the traditional, and charming African-style lodge.

ABOVE *Riders pause to take in the vast, silent majesty of the rolling landscape from a hill in the Lapalala Wilderness.*

Beyond the property, they also have access to neighbouring game farms as well as the nearby Lapalala Wilderness, one of the last true wilderness areas of South Africa. This private game reserve, established in 1985 by Clive Walker, covers an area of 18,000ha (44,478 acres) and encompasses 45km (28 miles) of the Palala River and its majestic gorge. The Lapalala is one of the last remaining strongholds of both black and white rhino; it also features large numbers of antelope, zebra, blue wildebeest, and an abundance of hippopotamuses and crocodiles in the waterways. There are also a number of historically and culturally significant sites, including a rock overhang adorned with ancient Bushmen paintings and a 6ha (15-acre) Iron-age settlement.

A personal desire to restore the Waterberg region to its pristine, naturally wild state is the motivation behind Equus, the oldest established horse safari company in South Africa. Owner Wendy Adams is a passionate naturalist with a genuine, contagious enthusiasm for all creatures, and a deep love of the African landscape. Wendy recently moved her entire horse-riding operation from a concession within the Lapalala Wilderness to her own patch of paradise, a 950ha (2347-acre) property at the top of the Kransberg peaks, the southernmost escarpment of the Waterberg range.

While she may have lost the opportunity to ride among big game such as endangered black and white rhino, for Wendy, there is nothing more rewarding than owning her own land. Not only is it less stressful, the black rhino were volatile riding companions to say the least, but she now has direct control over decision making and environmental change. Wendy's first mission was to tear down all the fences, creating a free-range environment for her horses and the indigenous wildlife, which becomes more prolific every day as the animals become accustomed to the sight of horses and riders. There are daily sightings of kudu, reedbuck, duiker, warthog and hundreds of baboon. Fresh leopard and hyena spoors are also regularly seen, and bird life is abundant, particularly near the central lodge overlooking a tranquil lily pond. The largest colony of endangered Cape vultures in Africa breed in the nearby Marakele National Park and these birds can often be seen hovering on thermals above the ridges on the reserve.

Equus also has traversing rights on more than 4500ha (10,845 acres) of neighbouring land where guests can observe zebra, wildebeest, impala and ostrich. With her neighbours' support, Wendy's goal is to work toward a local conservancy – a large protected area with no fenced boundaries, allowing game to wander without restrictions between properties. In the meantime, Wendy and her guests act as an antipoaching patrol in the area, reporting on any unusual sightings or any animals in distress.

The Equus Reserve falls within the UNESCO Waterberg Biosphere Reserve and incorporates over 414,000ha (1,023,000 acres) in the Limpopo Province. There are 320 such designated reserves around the world that establish an ethic of responsible land management. The endeavour is to tread lightly on the earth, to live in harmony with the natural environment – a philosophy fully embraced and qualified at Equus.

It is not only the wild game that benefits from these gentle environmental practices. Wendy's 20 or so horses are arguably the happiest creatures in the world, sweet-natured and enthusiastic with an unprecedented willingness to please. Her herd is a mix of Boerperd, Friesian, Arab and Warmblood crosses, all well trained, forward going and responsive. Riders are encouraged to

ABOVE RIGHT *The traditionally designed lodge at the new Equus Reserve provides a comfortable place to relax and socialize after hours in the saddle.*

ride English style in comfortable South African McClellan saddles. With magnificent open trails, the going can be fast with delightful kilometre-long canters demanding a reasonably high standard of riding ability.

The Boerperd is a South African breed whose origins can be traced back to 1652, when the first horses arrived at the Cape of Good Hope from the Dutch East Indies. These horses, featuring

Arab, Thoroughbred and Javanese pony bloodlines became known as the Cape Horse, which is renowned for its hardiness and resistance to tick-borne disease. Some of these animals were exported to Australia in 1788, forming the rootstock for the Australian Waler breed.

The Boerperd, as the Cape Horse came to be known, cemented its reputation during the military campaigns of the Boer Wars when it was praised for its endurance and level-headed behaviour in battle. Today, this stocky, sturdy little horse with its hogged mane and rounded quarters, is a wonderful trail horse. The animal is reliable, surefooted and unfazed by other

creatures sharing its grazing lands. To ride these honest creatures through an unspoiled African landscape is truly a journey of discovery. Every rock face and grove reveals a hidden treasure – a family of baboons barking a raucous challenge, the pricked ears of a curious reedbuck ready for flight, and the exuberant display of a long-tailed widow bird flitting around a spreading acacia bush. Even the diligent effort of a tiny dung beetle intrigues as it hauls its smelly burden, making a crucial contribution to the African ecosystem.

The highlight of any riding trek in the Waterberg, however, is the opportunity to simply pause and absorb the endless panorama. Under the shadow of the Kranz, which is the southernmost escarpment of the Equus Reserve, Africa lies before you – a vast patchwork of farmland and wilderness, an ever-changing kaleidoscope that encapsulates the complexity of this timeless land. This is Africa at its most majestic – silent, austere, a sentinel – truly a landscape of literature and dreams.

Okavango Delta, the Jewel of Africa

Okavango Delta, the Jewel of Africa

OKAVANGO, BOTSWANA

Location *Okavango Delta*

Getting there *Light aircraft from Maun to the nearest airstrip, then transfer to the camp*

Season *March–November*

Duration *6–11 days*

Group size *Maximum of 8 riders*

Horses *Thoroughbred, Anglo-Arab, Arab*

Tack *English*

Pace *Moderate to fast*

Riding ability *Intermediate to advanced*

WITH HIS TRUNK HELD HIGH AND EARS FLAPPING frantically, I knew enough about interspecies body language to know that this bull elephant was not in the mood for socializing. It was at about this time that I started to regret asking for a docile horse – Linyati, unfazed by yet another boring elephant sighting had dropped his head to graze, tearing at the long, golden grass without a care in the world. In the meantime, PJ was edging closer and closer to the cranky beast, motioning to me silently to take a photo. Never have I been so nervous, so delighted, and so aware of every fibre of my being, from racing pulse to sweating palms. My hands trembled as I squeezed the shutter on my camera, the buzzing automatic wind-on shattering the silence. My heart was in my throat; my eyes filled with tears.

For nature lovers, there is surely no greater thrill than a close-up encounter with the astonishing wildlife of Africa. I feel privileged to have fulfilled a life-long dream, and blessed that I did so from the best vantage point in the world – from the back of a horse.

This is surely the ultimate method of game viewing. Roaring across rutted tracks in a 4x4 may be fast and efficient, but the animals will always hear you coming and bid a hasty retreat. On a horse, the approach is silent and intense. Unencumbered by physical barriers of glass and steel, you become part of the landscape, at one with its wildlife. You are a participant in the environment, not just a casual observer.

From a safety perspective, horseback safaris are also superior to those conducted on foot. Not only does the extra elevation provide a great viewing platform, but there is the obvious advantage of speed in the necessity of a quick getaway. Which does happen – often. In the case of our encounter with the gnarly bull elephant, our guide PJ Bestelink knew exactly when to call it a day. Once alerted to our scent, the elephant's nervous stance had turned to aggression, ears flapping and trunk raised as a warning of his might. One menacing step forward – and PJ chose to retreat, signalling for us to walk off quietly and orderly. When confronted with a giant of the African bush, there is no room for argument.

Horse riding in itself is inherently dangerous, even more so when riding among unpredictable wildlife. For this reason, safety is of paramount importance at Okavango Horse Safaris. Rides are always accompanied by at least two experienced guides, both armed with bearbangers – a pen-sized device which shoots a loud, explosive pellet. A .357 rifle is also carried, more for peace of mind than necessity – to date, it has never been used. Before embarking on a trek, guests are given a detailed safety rundown; they are then carefully matched with their horses, according to their ability.

Most importantly, PJ and his wife, Barney, insist that their guests are all experienced horse riders – competent, confident and capable of galloping out of trouble if necessary. This is definitely not a sightseeing trip for beginners, which is made quite clear from the moment of inquiry.

Okavango Horse Safaris is based on 2500 square kilometres (965 square miles) of private

---

ABOVE LEFT *The enormous delta of the Okavango River expands into a watery wonderland during the annual flood.*

OPPOSITE *A view from the saddle at a water hole at Macateers Camp, one of two permanent campsites used on the Okavango Horse Safari.*

concession on the edge of the Moremi Game Reserve, a short charter flight from Maun. This is pure wilderness – there are no fences, no tarred roads, no telephone lines, and no sign of other human habitation.

The safari camp is entirely self-contained – power is provided by solar panels and meals are prepared in a traditional earthenware oven. An electric fence surrounds the whole compound to protect its human and equine inhabitants from prowling wildlife.

Despite its isolation, the base camp of Kujwana couldn't be more comfortable. Nestled among wild fig and sausage trees riddled with raucous baboons and cheeky monkeys, the camp overlooks a permanent pool on the Xudum river system, a serene location offering glorious views of sunrise and sunset.

Large safari-style canvas tents on raised decks provide sleeping quarters for two, with flushing toilets and hot running water, definitely a welcome surprise. Meals are always fresh and delicious, and an endless supply of cold beer and wine with which to relax after a long day in the saddle. With only eight guests catered for per week, a riding holiday in the delta is an intimate affair, with PJ and Barney providing hours of

entertainment as they share tales of their bush exploits around a roaring campfire.

Treks are generally conducted early in the morning, when the wildlife is most active and visible. There is no set route – the four-hour rides are determined by the presence of game. Following freshly carved elephant highways, the group skirts around palm islands and lagoons, across plains of aromatic sage and turpentine grasses, and through the golden expanse of the *malopos*, the wide channels that fill with water during the flood. Returning to camp by lunchtime, the afternoon is dedicated to relaxation, followed by a jeep safari and 'sundowner' drinks by a lake. The encroaching darkness draws out a myriad of wild creatures seeking the protective cover of night.

In terms of wildlife sightings, Botswana's Okavango Delta is one of the richest treasure troves in Africa, a worthy recipient of the title 'the Jewel of Africa'. This enormous wetland is an oasis in the heart of one of the harshest deserts on earth, teeming with animal and bird life that flock to its life-giving waters and abundant feeding grounds. Lions, cheetahs and packs of wild dogs hunt on the open veldt; giraffe gracefully browse among the tree tops; while herds of wildebeest, buffalo and zebra congregate on flood plains surrounding permanent water holes. The bird life here is also incredibly rich and varied, with over 500 species on record.

This veritable 'Garden of Eden' is an oddity of nature. The Okavango River rises at the end of the rainy season, trickling south from Angola like a leaky garden hose, spreading like an open palm and swelling into floodwaters before being consumed by the dry air and the thirsty sands of the Kalahari. Often described as the 'river that never reaches the sea', the Okavango is consumed in a maze of lagoons, islands and channels covering an area of around 13,000 square kilometres (5000 square miles), a watery wilderness of crystal pools, shallow reed beds and islands of towering palm trees.

This annual miracle occurs between April and October; after that, the waters begin to recede. Paradoxically, the lowest water levels occur during the wet season (from November to March) when the game disperses over the rich grasslands. Most lodges close during this time, reopening when the weather is more reliable and the game more concentrated.

Purely from a riding perspective, the most fascinating time to visit Botswana's Okavango Delta is between July and September when the water level is still high.

With deep channels to swim and soft ground underfoot, the going can be challenging, but the exhilaration of hitting a lily-covered lagoon at a full gallop, water spraying under flailing hooves is incomparable – it truly is the riding experience of a lifetime.

LEFT *Horse and rider stretch out through the waist-deep grass of the* malopo *channels during Botswana's dry season.*

surveying the situation with his well-trained, observant bushranger's eye.

Camouflaged among the sea of gold were three huge heads – two lionesses and the ruffled mane of a juvenile male. We were later to discover that these three were well known amongst researchers, a renegade female and her two adolescent cubs who had severed ties with the main pride and were hunting alone. Being territorial as well as lazy creatures, lions do not wander far in search of prey, they simply wait for whatever crosses their path.

And there we were, eight entrées, readily available and all in one delicious package.

As the lions' curiosity turned to active interest, PJ and Barney rode off slowly at an angle, bear-bangers drawn in anticipation. Our hosts' caution was well founded – the young male was now in stalking mode, slinking through the grass in an attempt to round the group up from behind.

I, of course, was in my usual position at the rear – documentary images of the slowest zebra dragged to a gory death flashing through my mind. 'This is no time to eat,' I muttered to lazy Linyati, prodding him in the ribs with my boot. 'Keep up, no dawdling!' My heart pounded with sheer terror, my hands trembled and sweat trickled down my face; would the lions be able to sense my fear, and target me as easy prey?

Crossing that kilometre of open plain under the hungry gaze of the King of the Jungle was probably the most excruciating, adrenaline-pumping twenty minutes of my life! I swear I didn't draw breath until we were well out of danger, Barney visibly relaxing and laughing with relief as she put her bearbanger back in its holder.

Then, of course, came the obligatory 'near-miss' stories of a lioness lunging at PJ as he made a similar escape, or of the time his jeep broke down and he was forced to scramble up a tree for safety. These jaw-dropping tales always make great campfire entertainment – I was just relieved that I didn't have one to tell.

The daily challenges of the African bush are clearly an elixir of life for PJ Bestelink. This Namibian-born geologist has spent a lifetime delving into its intricacies, and his passion for the flora and fauna of the Okavango Delta is

There is also great appeal in visiting just prior to the flood, when the vast grasslands invite long, gleeful gallops among herds of zebra, giraffe, tsessebe and lechwe. At permanent waterholes, hippos congregate in stagnant pools, protecting the precious liquid from marauding crocodiles and warthog families wallowing on the muddy banks. Meanwhile, among waist-high golden grasses, prides of lion doze in the sun, waiting opportunistically for migrating herds of buffalo and antelope to pass their way.

An idyllic scene indeed – until we stumbled across it on foot, leading our horses during a well-deserved break. As we rounded a clearing on the edge of a palm island, one of our sharp-eyed African grooms softly uttered one terrifying word – 'lion'. Breaking all world mounting records, I flung myself into the saddle and prepared for flight. 'Just sit quietly,' warned PJ,

ABOVE *Observing wild animals without the physical barrier of a motorized vehicle provides the ultimate horse-riding thrill!*

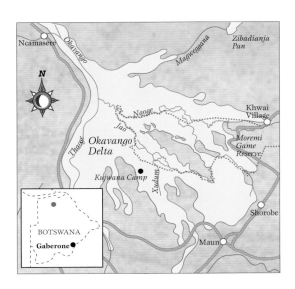

contagious. His sharp eyes never miss a detail – a leopard spoor in the sand, a marula tree stripped bare by an elephant, a vulture soaring above a freshly killed carcass. Every creature fascinates and delights – this wiry frontier cowboy obviously loves his job and his adopted homeland.

Complementing this boundless enthusiasm is Barney's dedication to her beloved horses, a factor that makes the Okavango Horse Safari one of the most applauded horse treks in the world. It's not easy to keep 60 horses in this harsh environment – veterinarians and farriers are hard to come by, hard feed has to be trucked in from South Africa, and the horses must be stabled and protected around the clock from prowling carnivores.

It is testament to Barney's horse husbandry that her team remains in good condition – sleek, fit and educated. Many of them are Thoroughbreds – some are ex-racehorses that were rescued from Zimbabwe – all have adapted well to life in the bush, taking the new sights, smells and sounds in their stride.

This is also the challenge for Okavango Horse Safari guests, to sharpen their senses and absorb the nuances of the African wilderness. After six days without the distractions of

ABOVE *Splashing through a reed-filled lagoon at sunset – a colourful and romantic end to a long day in the saddle.*

cellular (mobile) phones, televisions or traffic, eyes and ears suddenly tune in to a secret world, one that at first had appeared silent and empty. Shadows on an extensive plain become a mighty herd of buffalo, a dull sound of stampeding through the night. An endless horizon reveals the bobbing heads of passing giraffes, and an empty lake disguises a kaleidoscope of curious eyes.

For me, the biggest awakening of all came courtesy of Linyati, my trusty four-legged safari companion. The natural act of grazing, the gentle rise and fall of his head as he chewed on the golden grass was a signal to both man and beast to relax, to simply enjoy the moment. It was wise advice indeed.

Masai Mara Safari

𝓜asai Mara Safari
KENYA, EAST AFRICA

Location *Deloraine*

Getting there *Car transfers from Nairobi (2.5-hour drive)*

Season *January–March; June–October*

Duration *11–14 days*

Group size *Minimum of 4; maximum of 12 riders*

Horses *Somali, Thoroughbred*

Tack *English*

Pace *Moderate to fast*

Riding ability *Intermediate to advanced*

Horse people tend to be pretty tough. We are no strangers to hard work, and we're not afraid of getting dirty. The simple act of sitting on a horse in itself requires courage, determination and nerves of steel. New challenges are part of our daily existence.

Then there are those who push these boundaries even further, embarking on horse-riding adventures in faraway, exotic places. These people are a special breed, revelling in new experiences, opening their minds and souls to the infinite wonders of the universe. This often requires throwing caution to the wind, pushing your body to its limits, and overcoming innate fears. It may require transgressing your comfort zone, but the rewards for doing so are immeasurable. These are life-enriching experiences – adventures that give purpose to existence on this earthly realm.

Imagine, for instance, sitting on the back of a horse with the grassy plains of eastern Africa spread before you. To your left is a herd of zebra cautiously grazing, ears pricked, ever alert to danger. On your right is a sea of wildebeest interspersed with the bobbing tails and curved horns of myriad antelopes. In the distance, a nursery of elephants makes its ponderous way to the riverbank, while amongst the grasses predators hide patiently, undetected, waiting for the opportunity to strike at the weak. You have become a part of the greatest wildlife show on earth – the annual migration of the wildebeest in their relentless search for greener pastures, an endless cycle of life and death.

This may well be the riding opportunity of a lifetime, the chance to witness one of the planet's greatest natural phenomena. Many who have undertaken a horse safari in the Masai Mara region of Kenya claim it to be the most exciting and rewarding trek of all, a combination of great scenery, excellent riding, fascinating cultural exchanges and unparalleled game viewing.

These rides are not for everyone, however; there are certainly easier places to visit which are cheaper, safer and less nerve-racking. Positioned in the heart of East Africa, bordered by countries of fluctuating economic and political stability, Kenya itself can be a volatile destination. Many governments are warning of potential dangers and currently discouraging travel to its capital, Nairobi.

Hazards of a different kind exist in Kenya's vast wilderness. Horseback safaris take you beyond the comforts of resorts and safari lodges, far from fences, roads, telephones and flushing toilets. Out here, hundreds of miles from civilization, you become part of the landscape, and as vulnerable as the wildlife you have come to see. The dangers can be very real!

With vast open plains to traverse, the going can be fast and furious. Riders need to be experienced and prepared for long, gruelling hours in the saddle. They must be competent at all paces, and confident enough to gallop out of danger if necessary. Once they are out here, there is no turning back.

Statistically, of course, the dangers are minimal – I believe, however, that people should be

---

ABOVE LEFT *A group of riders eagerly sets off on their ride in Masai Mara National Park to witness the annual migration of the wildebeest on horseback.*

OPPOSITE *Interaction and cultural exchange with the local Maasai people add a unique and fascinating dimension to a ride in Kenya.*

aware of the possible dangers when riding in the wild. This is a true adventure that requires stamina and courage. Only the intrepid need apply.

There are two major players in Kenya's horse safari market: Tony Church, who pioneered long-distance riding treks in 1972, and his protégé Tristan Voorspuy, who established Offbeat Safaris in 1990. Both are renowned for their horsemanship, knowledge of the bush and hospitality; and both companies have a reputation for fast, exciting rides.

Tristan Voorspuy, a former British army officer, is a keen polo player who fosters his string of 40 polo ponies in sumptuous surrounds at Deloraine – a three-hour drive from Nairobi brings you to this magnificent colonial estate which lies on the western edge of the Rift Valley.

ABOVE *The sun sets over the Masai Mara National Park as a horse-riding group approaches their campsite.*

With its wide verandas and manicured gardens, Deloraine is one of the grand homes of Kenya, a showpiece built in 1920 by the prominent early settler, Lord Francis Scott. An overnight stay at the beginning or end of the safari provides guests with a taste of colonial history and hospitality, bringing to life the romance of Isak Dinesen and Ernest Hemingway's Africa.

Once the safari begins in earnest, however, things become a little less salubrious – though certainly far from rustic. Accommodation is in

two-person tents furnished with comfortable single beds freshly made each day. Several toilet and shower sheds are also set up, with hot water always on the boil. Cold beer and fine South African wines beckon at the end of a long day in the saddle, and gourmet-quality meals are freshly prepared and served by uniformed waiters. One could call it the camping version of the Ritz – roughing it has never been quite so grand!

As darkness descends, a roaring fire is a welcome barrier between camp and the nocturnal mysteries of the African bush. Under the starry Southern sky every sound is amplified, from the shrill cry of a bush baby and the call of a zebra to the chilling roar of a lion on the hunt. With this cacophony of bizarre noises, sleep doesn't always come easy, your senses awakened despite physical exhaustion.

Tending to the fires and watching over the tethered horses are two Maasai warriors, guarding the camp against marauding lions. After

generations of living in harmony with the wildlife, it seems that the Maasai have the upper hand, the lions warily keeping their distance from these imposing, silent sentries with their dramatic red capes and impressive spears.

Once nomadic warriors, the tall, slender Maasai are now the custodians of this great wilderness, living in simple villages and tending to their cattle, sheep and goats in the traditional manner, sometimes herding them for hundreds of kilometres in search of rich grazing pastures.

Centuries ago, these people were feared as ruthless conquerors, invading other tribal areas in search of more cattle, which they believed they had exclusive rights to. Cattle still form the basis of the traditional Maasai way of life.

ABOVE *A group of riders experiences the wildlife of Africa, as a herd of tsessebe bound across their path in the Masai Mara National Park.*

Their diet is based on a mixture of meat, curdled milk and blood taken from the cow in a unique blood-letting ceremony. This sounds more violent than it really is – while one holds the chosen beast by the nose another shoots an arrow from close range into the jugular vein, the protein-rich liquid spurting into a skin gourd. The procedure is swift and deft, and the cow's wound is carefully tended, rapidly clotting and healing.

The opportunity to interact with the proud Maasai tribespeople adds another dimension to the Kenyan riding experience. Riders are welcomed into *manyattas*, the traditional villages, where they can buy trinkets and beads, and take a closer look at the cow-dung huts and the animal pens made from thorns, as well as witness the daily activities such as milking the cows.

The 'real' Offbeat trek commences in remote country near the Tanzanian border on the Liota Hills overlooking the Serengeti. After spending

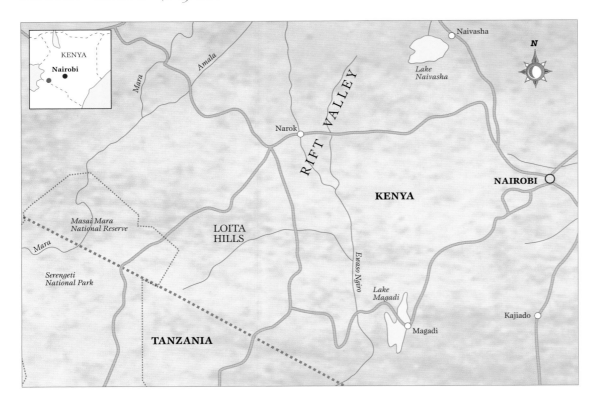

a few days exploring this densely forested country, the ride moves off toward the Bardamat Hills, crossing plains with ever-increasing numbers of wildlife.

Here, the close-cropped pastures cry out for a canter and the inevitable headlong gallop, herds of zebra and wildebeest cutting in as they join the joyful cavalcade. This is arguably the most exhilarating riding experience in the world, as exciting and liberating for the horse as it is for the rider – words cannot express just how wonderful this can make you feel!

Tristan's polo ponies, mostly homebred Thoroughbreds crossed with Somali Arabs for endurance, seem to relish the opportunity to stretch out, agilely dodging holes in complete mastery of the terrain. These horses are fit and well schooled, galloping tirelessly for two or three miles and barely raising a sweat. It is testament to the operator's dedication and care of his horses that they remain in top condition in the difficult East Africa conditions.

The Masai Mara Safari is different. Every few days, the camp moves closer toward its final destination. Bayard Fox, who also experienced this ride, said, 'Day after day we rode on and the camp we left was moved again, only magically to reappear at the end of the day, when we rode in hot and tired to find everything ready under a new set of those lovely, spreading acacias with their feathery leaves. Bush babies and hyrax played in them over our heads at night. Each day held new adventures and new sights. We saw dozens of soft-eyed giraffes towering high into the air, often above the trees. The horses would stand with their ears pricked, staring at these incredible animals with their long necks and huge strides, which make them appear to be in slow motion at a gallop although they are really moving fast...'

After several days in untainted wilderness, covering up to 50km (31 miles) a day with no fences or roads to hinder progress, the ride finally reaches the Mara River and its incredibly complex and rich ecosystem. Here, the daily routine changes somewhat as the horses are given a well-earned rest and riders board a Land Rover for a safari into the heart of the game reserve where domestic animals are forbidden. At the height of the wildebeest migration, this is a dramatic spectacle with an astonishing number of species on display, plus guaranteed sightings of large cats on the prowl. The Masai Mara is considered the ultimate game park in Kenya.

Teeming with wild animals, Masai Mara's sweeping plains fulfil every Out of Africa fantasy. Gazetted in 1961, the reserve is a natural extension of the Serengeti Plains in Tanzania, bordered by the chocolate-coloured waters of the Mara River.

It is estimated that over one million wildebeest make the pilgrimage north each year, fording the river in their endless quest for rich pastures. In their wake follow countless other

herd creatures – impala, eland, gazelle, topi and 200,000 zebra – plus the large carnivores who relish the movable feast. When the herds cross the swollen river many of them drown in the raging waters, or are picked off by opportunistic crocodiles that lie in wait for beasts floundering on the muddy banks.

The peak time to view this spectacle is around August; the herds then graze on the verdant Mara plains before returning to the Serengeti with the November rains – the cycle of life continuing for another season.

The campsite on the escarpment overlooking the Serengeti is arguably the most evocative of all sights on this safari, a location described by my friend Bayard Fox as 'one of the world's glorious places which brings exultation to my soul in a way no cathedral ever could.' From an elevation of around 305m (1000ft), the vastness of the Mara Plains stretches before you, hazy shades of gold, blue and purple, a serene patchwork embellished with the gentle forms of grazing wildlife. This is a snapshot of wild Africa, a place of unadulterated wilderness – a treasure to be preserved and cherished by mankind.

ABOVE *Horses are tied to an overhead picket line while they feed from nosebags and receive a last-minute check before setting out on a ride.*

Asia

Palaces and Forts of Rajasthan

Palaces and Forts of Rajasthan
RAJASTHAN, INDIA

Location *Dundlod*

Getting there *Arrive in Delhi, and transfer south by bus to Dundlod*

Season *October–February*

Duration *3–12 days*

Group size *8–14 riders*

Horses *Marwari*

Tack *English. Indian military*

Pace *Moderate to fast*

Riding ability *Experienced*

THE PACE WAS RELENTLESS, A HEADLONG GALLOP along a dusty trail edged by boxthorn fences. My dun Marwari pony stretched bravely in a bid to keep up with Bonnie's magnificent paint mare, her curved ears twitching as she gave a little jolt, joyful at the speed and the soft ground underfoot. A protective mother squealed as we charged past, pulling her children to safety into the folds of her brilliant vermilion sari. Wide-eyed with curiosity the children peeked out, grins from ear to ear, shouting 'Namaste, hello, hello!' – a now familiar greeting, the warmest and most genuine welcome in the world.

For most Western visitors, India is a culture shock. This is a land of extremes – bedazzling riches and overwhelming poverty; ear-shattering noise and whispered inner peace; drabness and vivid hues. Here, one billion souls jostle for space in a seething sea of humanity, a bewildering kaleidoscope of colour, sound and aromas which confuse and disorientate, then entice and enchant.

To explore this dizzying subcontinent is to fall headlong into a chaotic cauldron where every sense is assaulted and expanded. To do so on horseback is to blow one's mind completely!

India is a country better known for its holy cows than its divine horses. There are few stables in the country – only the very wealthy can afford the privilege of riding for pleasure. There is a strong equestrian focus within the army, which still maintains a working cavalry, and traditional horse sports such as polo have a

passionate following. For the majority of Indian citizens, however, horse riding is a pastime enjoyed only by an elite few.

Despite its restrictions in terms of facilities and numbers, India is a wonderful surprise for horse-loving adventurers. A handful of commercial horse safaris takes travellers far beyond the polluted, groping cities into the fascinating rural regions where the urban madness is tempered by timeless traditions and a peaceful way of life. Here, way off the beaten tourist track, one can get close to the heart of the subcontinent, experiencing the complexities of Indian life – its joys and sorrows – first hand.

The epicentre of India's horse culture is the desert state of Rajasthan, a parched and monotonous wasteland where 56.5 million people eke out a living in historic cities, simple villages and on rural farms. This is one of the poorest states in India, cursed by a harsh environment with drought regularly threatening the livelihoods of ordinary people.

The vistas here are stark with a cloudless hazy sky and sparse, spiky vegetation set upon a grey, dusty ground. Square fields fenced by boxthorns often lay barren in anticipation of the annual monsoon, which may never come in these times of climatic chaos. The villages, densely packed centres of commercial activity, are equally dusty with holy cows and camel carts competing with lorries for the narrow, potholed road space.

For all its natural drabness, however, Rajasthan is ablaze with the colours of a rich and exotic

PREVIOUS PAGES *Horses graze on the treeless banks of a lake overlooking the Kharkhiraa mountains.* ABOVE LEFT *The distinctive curved ears and noble bearing of a Marwari Horse.*

OPPOSITE *Riding in India provides an intimate insight into a fascinating history and culture, with the opportunity to explore ancient temples, forts and palaces.*

culture. Iridescent greens, canary yellows, chilli reds and electric blues abound in a sea of turbans and lavishly embroidered saris – the effect is simply dazzling, a joy to behold and reflective of the warmth and hospitality of its people.

This is particularly true in the northern region of Shekhawati, a place relatively undiscovered and untainted by tourism. Here, in the tiny village of Dundlod, you'll find the Royal Equestrian and Polo Centre, the only horse safari centre in the country to be recognized and affiliated with the Equestrian Federation of India. The stables are owned by the charming and handsome Kanwar Raghuvendra Singh, known to everyone as Bonnie.

In Shekhawati, to be a wealthy white tourist is a curiosity; to be a visitor on horseback is a miracle, a truly fascinating sight. At every village, riders are greeted with enthusiastic shouts and waves; sari-clad women giggle shyly at their daunting presence, and children dash across fields of mustard seed for a close-up view of the strangely dressed equestrians.

It is this effusive hospitality that makes riding in India a special experience, but what makes it a true adventure are the horses themselves.

The pampered equine stars at Bonnie's stables at Dundlod is the beautiful and enigmatic breed called the Marwari, a strain relatively unknown to the Western world and largely neglected in its native India. Bred as a warhorse for the ruling Rajput nobles in medieval Rajasthan, this horse, which has descended from Oriental stock, is fiery, proud and intelligent. The Marwari has a strong, arched neck and high head carriage, topped by distinctive lyre-shaped ears which, when pricked, form a perfect arch. The horse's fine, silky coat and long, dewy eyelashes are other evolutionary traits, designed to ease the burden of desert dwelling.

During medieval times, when the rule of the Rajputs was at its peak, the status of these warhorses was unparalleled. Heroic exploits were recorded in literature – tales of horses leaping onto elephants in attack, and other amazing feats of endurance, bravery and loyalty. The

BELOW *A 'red carpet' arrival ceremony at Dundlod Fort sets a tone of pomp and luxury for guests embarking on a riding safari.*

horse was declared divine and superior to all men. Accordingly, only the Rajput families and the ruling warrior caste were permitted to be associated with these exalted beasts.

With the arrival of colonial rule, however, these animals were rejected as being too showy, too undisciplined, and altogether 'un-British'. The breed declined into oblivion, even to the verge of extinction.

The Rajputs, themselves stripped of their privileges, remained loyal to their battle companions. In the 1930s, the late Maharaja Umaid Singh of Jodphur began buying up the horses he could identify as being representative of the breed. Raja Narinder Singh, the oldest living Mewar prince, also turned his hunting lodge on the outskirts of Udaipur into a breeding centre.

Bonnie Singh is also a man of considerable historic stature. He is the direct descendent of the Rajput ruler, Kesari Singh, who built the castle at Dundlod in 1750. Although he now has no official status, Bonnie, who still resides in the

ABOVE *An impeccably turned out riding group sets off through the harsh desert environment near the Aravalli Hills.*

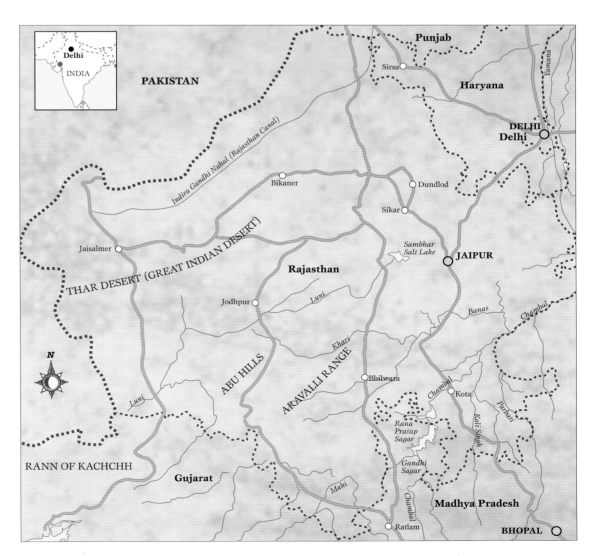

castle, is the undisputed leader of his community, and a champion of the humble folk of Dundlod.

Ten or so years ago, Bonnie, astute business-man that he is, jumped on the tourism band-wagon, converting his family fort into a heritage hotel, which is modestly luxurious with charm-ing rooms and an impeccable level of service on offer. As an added bonus, he cornered the riding safari market, attracting curious overseas visi-tors to this otherwise remote part of Rajasthan.

Bonnie's love affair with the Marwari Horse began in the 1980s, when he was the location scout for the Hollywood movie, *The Far Pavilions*. Filming was well under way before the movie producers realized an essential ele-ment was missing – authentic Indian horses. On behalf of the film company, Bonnie scoured the local area, finding 25 horses for the film. At the end of the filming, Bonnie found himself in pos-session of a whole stable of horses and a new obsession – the Marwari.

His stable is the largest breeding centre of Marwari Horses in the country, and his prized stallions and mares are being exported to the United States where they sell for over US$25,000.

Incredibly beautiful, Bonnie's riding horses are also hardy, fit and fast. The safari rides are conducted at a cracking pace, a command to 'trot' inevitably leading to a full-on gallop through the dunes for three or four, perhaps even more, kilometres at a time. For riders used to leisurely trails on a loose rein, this can be an exhausting, if exhilarating experience. Here, a high standard of horsemanship is mandatory, and riding fitness is a definite advantage. Long hours in the saddle combined with the furious pace make this a truly physical adventure.

Countering this, however, is the luxurious treatment you'll receive on the rides, beginning with a 'red carpet' traditional welcome at Dund-lod Fort. After an introductory ride around the surrounding dunes, guests head off on their safaris accompanied by an entourage of 30 staff

LEFT *Riding into the dusty sunset near Pushkar, the Dundlod flag proudly announces the arrival of another safari group into camp.*

members including grooms, chefs, tent pitchers and flag bearers carrying the colours of Dundlod.

A number of rides are available which explore the fascinating Shekhawati region and beyond. The most popular ride climaxes at the annual Pushkar Camel Fair, a colourful and historic event that attracts around 200,000 people and 50,000 animals each year. Smaller and less touristy is the local Naguar Fair, where many Marwari Horses exchange hands.

One of the highlights of riding in Shekhawati is the opportunity to explore *havelis*, or local mansions, decorated with beautiful frescoes. Once belonging to wealthy businessmen, many

ABOVE *Negotiations over the sale of a Marwari Horse at the Pushkar Fair, an annual event that attracts thousands of people.*

of these homes have fallen into disrepair, and are only now being appreciated and restored as fine works of art. The most magnificent of these *havelis* are found in the towns of Mandawa and Nawalgargh, though Dundlod itself has a number that are open to the public.

After exploring the towns and desert flats surrounding Bonnie's fort, the Pushkar Fair ride – held every year in late October to coincide with the famous camel fair – pushes on toward the magnificent 'Pink City' of Jaipur, the capital of Rajasthan. From here, the riders are transported by vehicle to observe the festivities of the fair. En route, the ride passes through farmland at the foothills of the Aravalli Hills with visits to various *havelis*, forts and temples such as the Bhairon Ji Temple, dedicated to the dark-faced idol of Bhairon who attracts mystics, snake charmers and those in search of *siddhi*, or enlightenment.

There are no 'orange and sandwich' breaks on Bonnie's rides; lunch consists of a three-course hot meal, delicious curries, and wine. And at the end of the day, there are comfortable beds set up in impressive Imperial Raj-style canvas tents – a cozy end to a wearying day in the saddle. The occasional night is also spent in the comfort of family-owned palaces and forts, converted into simple, romantic and highly evocative hotels.

Riding in India is not for the faint-hearted. The hours in the saddle are long and dusty, the horses are spirited and demand constant concentration, and conditions along the trail can be primitive. The rewards, however, are immeasurable: the joy of riding gallant and spirited horses while experiencing the genuine warmth of the Indian people, and an enriched understanding of a complex and fascinating culture.

Nomads of Khentii

Nomads of Khentii

KHENTII REGION, MONGOLIA

Location *Various parts of Mongolia*

Getting there *Transfers from Ulaan-baatar included*

Season *May–September*

Duration *14 days*

Group size *4–8 riders*

Horses *Mongolian horses*

Tack *Mongolian; Russian Cavalry*

Pace *Varies – can be fast*

Riding ability *Novice to advanced*

HORSE LOVERS ASSOCIATE RIDING WITH FREEDOM. The reality is, however, that in an urbanized Western world, our equestrian activities are becoming increasingly restricted. We trot around a dusty arena, jump under lights in an indoor stadium and potter around paddocks the size of handkerchiefs. We compete with cars and bikes for road space. If we're lucky, we'll venture onto a trail, often under the scrutiny of authorities that consider our presence an environmental threat – where has the freedom gone?

In horseman's heaven we ride under an endless sky, galloping for miles across verdant grasslands strewn with wildflowers, through mountain passes and along crystal streams. There are no fences to hinder our passage, no borders to slow our pace. There are no buildings or roads. There is no end in sight. This is riding as it should be; unfettered, unrestricted, at one with nature and the nature of the horse, an animal created for open spaces.

Such freedom does exist and this heaven has a name: Mongolia, the land of the horse. Here in this landlocked Asian country, the horse is an icon and an integral part of the culture, the embodiment of a nomadic lifestyle. Children are taught to ride when they are very young, and a man's status is measured by his skill as a horseman. To the Mongolians the horse represents more than just freedom, it is their mode of transport, a symbol of self and national identity and an indication of wealth. There is no other country in the world so closely associated with the horse.

Sandwiched between Russia in the north and China in the south, Mongolia is an intriguing and unexplored frontier, one of the last places in the world untainted by modern development. This is a large, underpopulated country with only 2.5 million inhabitants from over 15 distinct ethnic groups spread across 1,560,500 square kilometres (1,343,591 square miles) of desert, steppe and mountain terrain. With an average altitude of 1580m (5184ft) above sea level, it is one of the highest countries in the world.

Mongolia's 5000-year history is steeped in legend. The Hunnu people, who are the most powerful tribe in Central Asia, established the first Mongolian State in 209BC. In 1189, the 20-year-old warlord Genghis Khan rampaged across the steppes, uniting the 81 warring Mongolian tribes and thus created the largest land empire the world has ever known, stretching at its zenith from Southeast Asia to Finland. The key to their control was the speed, endurance and riding skills of their 200,000-strong cavalry, a legacy which has been passed down through generations.

The 20th century brought many changes to Mongolia; first, independence from the Manchurians who took control in 1691, then communism, which forced many people to move to the city and give up their nomadic way of life. With the collapse of the Soviet Union in 1990, however, the country has undergone a cultural revolution as old traditions have been revived. The people once again practise their favoured religion, Tibetan Buddhism, and horsemen again dominate the steppes.

ABOVE LEFT *A Mongolian nomad crosses a broad riverbed with his trusty equine companion and a train of camels.*

OPPOSITE *Extremes of temperature are a feature of the brief riding season in the remote Altai Mountains in Mongolia.*

Today, Mongolia is an independent country with a democratically elected parliament and president. It has embraced free-market economics with enthusiasm and is open to external influences, competition and global market trends.

Tourism is also still very much in its infancy in Mongolia and the associated infrastructure, hotels and services, is relatively undeveloped. Travelling around the country may be slow and sometimes frustrating, but this is countered by the rare opportunity to experience the simple, unspoiled and unique culture first-hand. Mongolians are warm, hospitable people who generously open their homes to strangers and enthusiastically share their traditions with curious visiting tourists.

There is no greater honour to the Mongolians than to share their love of horses with foreigners. Most tours include at least a day on horseback, usually riding with a family group. Specialist horse tours are also popular, exploring up to 80km (50 miles) a day on horseback.

Mongolians assume that Westerners cannot ride horses, and a responsible herder will take care to choose quiet mounts for his guests and pay great attention to safety whilst riding. Nonetheless, without language skills there is little by way of instruction in how to ride a Mongolian horse – raw beginners simply follow by example. This may involve learning the hard way, with many newcomers discovering that the biggest trick to riding a horse is actually staying in the saddle!

In the tradition of Genghis Khan's Golden Horde, riders, whether local or visiting tourists, are expected to trot and gallop for long

ABOVE LEFT *Riding comes naturally to Mongolian children, who learn about the importance of the horse from an early age.*

LEFT *Horses wait outside a traditional Mongolian* ger, *a wooden-framed tent made from felt.*

OPPOSITE *A group of Western tourists learn the basics of Mongolian horsemanship in the Altai Mountains. Despite the small stature of the Mongolian horses, they are never referred to as 'ponies'.*

periods, their Mongolian wranglers waving their arms and shouting encouragement as they gallop past. 'Choo' is the Mongolian equivalent to 'giddy-up', and the horses respond smartly to the phrase, moving off with enthusiasm. Apart from the odd marmot hole, there are no obstacles so the going is unrestricted.

Western visitors invariably baulk at the traditional Mongolian saddles, which are made from wood with an exaggerated pommel and cantle, and decorative buckles protruding from the sides. The saddle blanket consists of two thick pieces of felt, placed between the saddle and the horse's back, while a pillow is thrown on top for the comfort of the rider. Comfort, of course, is the key issue here and most visitors soon adopt the traditional way of riding; standing in the stirrups at all paces. This riding style once enabled Mongol archers to fire whilst at full gallop.

On tours hosted by agencies, Russian Cavalry saddles are also available which may be a little kinder to delicate rear ends.

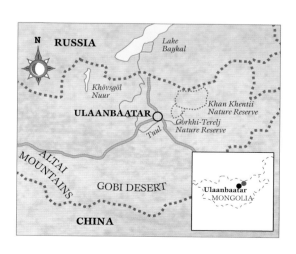

'manly sports' – wrestling, archery and horse racing. This nationwide festival centres in the capital of Ulaanbaatar, where the race is serious business indeed. Some herders ride for hundreds of miles to participate in the event while others go to the expense of transporting their horses by train or truck to avoid tiring them.

The horse races are the highlight of the event, with as many as a 1000 horses competing in a 30km (19-mile) gallop. The jockeys are tiny boys and girls aged between four and seven. During the race, they often abandon saddles and clothes to further lighten their horse's burden. As the first riders approach the finish, the mounted crowd joins in the revelry, galloping alongside the winner to the finish line. It is a fitting climax to an amazing endurance test, a unique celebration of a nation's obsession with horses.

Beyond the eclectic capital is a myriad of horse-riding terrain, each as wild and untamed as the next. To the south lies the fabled Gobi Desert, enticing horse riders with its windswept dunes. Approximately 800km (500 miles) north-west of Ulaanbaatar is Central Asia's deepest lake, the beautiful Khovsgol Nuur, surrounded by soaring mountains flanked with alpine forests. In the extreme west of the country, you can ride through the Altai Mountains, and interact with the Islamic Kazakh people; while in the north, you can camp with the 'reindeer people', and experience yet another unique Mongolian subculture.

The most characteristic landscape in Mongolia is the treeless steppe with its undulating grasslands stretching as far as the eye can see. In this vast emptiness, distance has no meaning – herdsmen navigate by the sun and a camp is invariably just 'over there'. Riding groups travel and live as the nomads do, sleeping and dining in *gers*, the traditional round wooden-framed tents covered in felt. Everyday, the *gers* are disassembled and carried along with the luggage, either by yak cart or camel to the next campsite.

Mongolia boasts around 2.5 million horses, a ratio of 1:1 per head of population. They are descended from the wild Przewalski Horse, and are similarly short, stocky and tough enough to endure the harshest winters. The horses are broken in at two years of age, after which they join the riding herd. They wear no shoes, are rarely groomed and their grass diet is not supplemented with hard feed. Despite this, they are willing and able to carry a full-sized adult for miles on end, day after day, usually travelling at a furious pace that would leave most English thoroughbreds floundering.

Horses can be rented anywhere, from anyone and some tourists simply hook up with tour representatives touting for business in hotels. The rate is negotiated on the spot, and usually includes the hire of a horse, services of a guide who may or may not speak English, and accommodation within the family tented compound.

Those who like to travel with set schedules and some degree of organization may prefer to book their Mongolian rides with specialist agencies. These agents look after all insured goods, offer English-speaking guides who know the destination intimately, and guarantee that the rides are conducted through reputable establishments with good safety records. These services may cost more, but in return, you will have the assurance of dealing with a company that offers a professional infrastructure.

With a short, mild summer, the riding season in Mongolia is brief. Most visitors plan their tours to coincide with July's spectacular Naadam Festival, where Mongolian culture is celebrated in a display of the three traditional

ABOVE LEFT *A small group of local nomadic herdsmen proudly ride their tough, sturdy horses in the Kharkhiraa mountains.*

One of the most popular and accessible riding routes begins on the steppes and culminates in the densely forested Khan Khentii Protected Area northeast of Ulaanbaatar, the only true wilderness region in Mongolia. No people or domestic animals dwell here; it is the realm of herds of musk deer, moose, wild boar, brown bears and wolves. This area, the interior of the Gorkhi Terelj National Park, is spectacularly beautiful with running streams, deep, mysterious larch forests and panoramic views from sky-scraping mountain ridges. Camp is usually made further north in Jalman Meadows, a semi-permanent *ger* camp which is situated on a wildflower-blanketed meadow along the banks of the Tuul River.

The highlight of any Mongolian riding trek is interaction with local herdsmen, who are very often relatives or friends of the riding guides. On the appearance of the strange Western entourage, they will often drop their herding duties and ride alongside the group in appreciative curiosity. Riders are welcomed into nearby *gers*, where they are honoured with local delicacies such as clotted cream, glasses of homemade vodka and bowls of *airak* – fermented mare's milk – which is said to be great for skin, hair and even the libido.

A Mongolian horse trek is not for those who insist on their creature comforts, however. This is the Wild East – the tent accommodation is basic and the food, consisting of mutton in various guises, can be monotonous. Vegetables are hard to come by. There is obviously no power for razors or hair dryers. There may be a solar shower at camp, or you may just have to brave the icy waters of the river or lake. Toilets may or may not be screened – and, unfortunately, there are few trees for pit stops!

However, for those who can appreciate that they are in a different world, the rewards of this simple lifestyle are without comparison. This is more than just an amazing equine experience; by embarking on a Mongolian horse trek, you are choosing the life of the nomad, immersing yourself in a way of life which has remained unchanged since the awe-inspiring conquests of Genghis Khan, one of the greatest horsemen of all time.

BELOW *Horseback riding along the shores of Khovsgol Nuur, one of the most picturesque locations in Mongolia.*

Snowy Mountains High Country

Snowy Mountains High Country
VICTORIA, AUSTRALIA

Location *High Country of Victoria and NSW*

Getting there *5-hour drive from Melbourne to Anglers Rest, Victoria; 6-hour drive from Sydney to Adaminaby*

Season *October–April*

Duration *3–6 days*

Group size *Minimum 2; maximum of 8 riders*

Horses *Australian Stock Horse, Thoroughbred, some mixed breed and brumbies*

Tack *Australian stock saddles; English*

Pace *Moderate*

Riding ability *Novice to advanced*

IT WAS ONE OF THOSE SPELLBINDING MOMENTS, when time is suspended and hearts, both human and animal, momentarily stop before pounding triple time with adrenaline. Deep in the heart of the Kosciuszko wilderness, a grey brumby stallion emerged from a eucalyptus grove, teeth bared in defiance, challenging a group of horseback riders who dared to venture into his territory, too close to his precious band of mares. He loomed larger than life – this creature is a legend from the pages of literature. Then, in an instant, he vanished with no trace but the faint imprint of hooves and the rustle of the wind to herald his fleeting presence.

A ghostly vision, and the very essence of riding in the Australian bush. This ancient, pristine wilderness is the spiritual heart of the continent, a place where the Dreamtime legends of the Aboriginals start to make sense and the stories of pioneers are brought to life. Here, the mythologies of the 19th-century bush poet Banjo Paterson, so beloved by the Australian people, become reality – a place where the men are rugged and courteous, the horses surefooted and true, and the beer is always cold!

It's also a world of extremes – of overwhelming solitude and intense conversation; of lofty heights and vast plains; of strange and curious wildlife; of drought, bushfires and floods. It's a world entrenched in the Australian psyche, yet experienced by so few, which is what makes delving deep into its soul on horseback such a special experience.

The scale of Australia's wilderness is difficult to comprehend. Some national parks cover millions of hectares; there are even cattle stations belonging to single families that are the size of small European nations. Australia is a huge, underdeveloped country!

When the first white settlers arrived on these shores 200 years ago, the only way to explore this formidable countryside was on horseback. Little has changed. While cars may shuttle you quickly around the perimeters of national parks and forests, the only way of getting into some areas is by foot, whether two or four. Even that is becoming more and more difficult as national-park authorities restrict leisure activities to protect the fragile environment. In some states, horse riding is banned in defined wilderness regions; there is even talk of re-routing the Bicentennial National Trail, a 5330km (3312-mile) trekking route that runs the entire length of the east coast of Australia, in order to avoid the national parks.

Bureaucracies aside, horse riding is still the best way to get up close and personal with Australia's unique landscapes.

It takes a special kind of horse to endure this country's extremes, and Australia does indeed have special horses – tough as nails, bred out of hardship for hardship. Horses are not native to this land – they arrived with the convicts in 1788; a handful of 'unattractive' horses from the Cape of Good Hope, of English and Spanish descent. The strongest horses were retained for

PREVIOUS PAGES *Two cattle workers are saddled up, and ready to roundup their herd in the Snowy Mountains.*
ABOVE LEFT *A group of riders puts their faith in*

their mounts as they cross a swollen river.
OPPOSITE *Without hesitation, a High Country rider charges through a river on his surefooted stock horse, trusty cattle dog in hot pursuit.*

breeding, and despite their mixed origins, they developed into a handsome type known as the Waler, acclaimed as the finest cavalry horses in the world during the Indian Mutiny, the Boer War and World War I.

When you visit Australia on a horse-trekking vacation, this is the type of horse you are likely to ride – a true snaffle-bit horse now known as the Australian Stock Horse. For long-distance riding, they are unsurpassed – chosen by horse-riding operators for their level-headed nature, stamina and surefootedness over uneven ground. Other breeds you'll encounter include Thoroughbreds, Arab derivatives and Clydesdale crosses – you may even find a purebred brumby among the herd. Brumbies are feral horses that have been captured and domesticated, often with great success.

In the Snowy Mountains, some of the most reliable trail horses once ran with the brumbies; they now plod happily along under saddle, unperturbed by the sight of the wild brumbies running free.

Like their American counterparts, the mustangs, brumbies are descended from horses that either escaped or were set free into the Australian bushland, where they flourished and multiplied. Today, it is estimated that there are between 300,000 and 600,000 brumbies in the Australian bush; however, that number is declining as eradication programmes are implemented by government authorities that consider the wild horses an environmental nuisance.

In the meantime, encounters with the brumbies are a definite highlight of many wilderness treks in Australia, especially those in the New South Wales (NSW) and Victorian High Country. This magnificent alpine region, spread out over 1,600,000ha (3,953,600 acres) across three states and territories, offers perhaps the quintessential Australian riding experience, one which fulfils fantasies of adventure, magnificent vistas, wide open plains, starry skies and cozy campfires – ingredients of every memorable horse ride!

RIGHT *A herd of brumbies – the legendary wild horses of the Snowy Mountains High Country – gallops through a glade of snow gums.*

By world standards, the peaks of the Australian Alps are mere pimples, with the tallest, Mount Kosciuszko, clocking in at just 2228m (7352ft). In a flat, dry continent with an average altitude of just 300m (984ft), however, these mountains are quite significant, with a cooler, moister climate than the rest of the continent. This is the only part of Australia where it snows regularly during winter, and despite the diminutive scale of the peaks, this region has more snow-covered terrain than Switzerland.

In the warmer months between October and April, however, the alpine High Country is an achingly beautiful destination for horse riders and bushwalkers who delight in endless panoramas of wildflower-studded grasslands, dramatic rocky outcrops, crystal-clear streams and groves of stark snow gums contorted into surreal knots by winter's icy winds and snowdrifts.

While the rest of the continent swelters in the summer haze, the alpine region is generally quite temperate, with warm sunny days and refreshingly cool nights. Riders must be prepared, however, for extremes – at these altitudes, the weather can turn at any moment, and it is not beyond the realm of possibility for a freak summer snowstorm to be followed by an oppressive heatwave. As the locals say, 'One day it's perfect, the next it's trying to kill you'. Most operators provide their clients with Driza-Bones®, impressive and stylish ankle-length oilskin riding coats, traditionally worn by cattlemen in the High Country but adopted by many Australians as a 'wet-weather' fashion statement.

Unfortunately, another 'Aussie' icon, the famous Akubra hat – perfect for keeping the sun off your face, the rain off your neck and your horse well-watered – has recently been deemed unacceptable in terms of safety; all horse-riding clients must now wear regulation helmets.

Choosing a High Country ride may very well depend on where you are based. The southernmost part of the Victorian Alps, for instance, is only a two-hour drive from Melbourne, making the rides out of Mansfield and Mount Buller extremely accessible. This is a beautiful part of the world, rugged and dramatic, and whilst a long way from the Snowy River, it was the

location chosen to represent the legend in the film version of *The Man From Snowy River*.

Riders who have seen the movie and want to visit recognizable landmarks such as Craig's Hut, or the eerily named Hell's Window, may be more than satisfied with riding the trails in this region. Accessibility, however, also means commercialism. If you are after a true wilderness experience, far from the madding busloads and day-trippers, you may prefer to head deeper and higher into the mountains.

During winter months, the ski resorts of Mount Hotham and Falls Creek are lively party towns; in summer, they are mere ghost towns with only a few dedicated bushwalkers and nature lovers keeping businesses afloat. For riders exploring this region, known as the Bogong High Plains, the silence is golden, and groups can be assured of absolute privacy and solitude as they venture off the beaten track.

Nestled among lush grazing pastures on the banks of the remote Bundarrah River is The Willows, a delightful retreat providing the base for some of the most exhilarating and authentic High Country riding in Victoria. The Willows is a country 'home away from home' – hosts, Helen and Russell are intelligent, entertaining and gracious. The pioneer-style accommodation

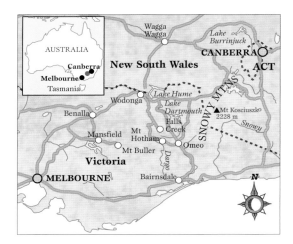

is eclectic and rustic, and the rural setting couldn't be more picturesque. The casual, warm ambience is enhanced by the close proximity of one of the best little pubs in Australia, The Blue Duck Inn at Anglers Rest, renowned for its great food, cold beer and quirky characters.

A variety of rides is available from The Willows, from day rides exploring the surrounding farmlands and bushland to extended multi-day treks into the Alpine National Park and back through the Glen Valley. Following tracks forged by kangaroos and brumbies, the rides crisscross pristine rivers, climb spurs of dry forest and weave around ancient granite boulders

to spectacular vistas overlooking the Mitta River and the surrounding Bogong mountains – a vast panorama seemingly untouched by human hands.

This welcome absence of civilization is countered by an abundance of wildlife – kangaroos in flight as hoof beats approach, bounding away in spectacular style; wallabies grazing peacefully along river flats in the evening light; dingoes, the much-maligned Australian wild dog, slinking along pebbly creek beds in search of prey; eagles, sublime lords of the air. Other animals, more elusive, make their presence felt in other ways – wombat holes and huge underground caverns of freshly dug earth are a constant hazard for delicate equine legs stretched at a gallop. It's a cavalcade of exotica, a fascinating biology lesson for overseas visitors and locals alike.

It takes at least a day of constant riding – usually uphill through glades of gnarled snow gums, to reach areas of total isolation. It's a tough call for horses and riders alike, with long hours in the saddle putting real pressure on knees, backs and rear ends. The horses, mountain-bred and trail-fit, seem to cope exceptionally well, regaining their energy once the grade flattens.

Extended treks into the High Country are not for the faint-hearted. Each day consists of at least six gruelling hours in the saddle; accommodation is in tents, or swags rolled out under the stars. Meals are cooked around a campfire – hearty country fare and billy tea. Bathroom facilities consist of the bush, and riders bathe in the nearest river, creek or dam. There's nothing quite like a brisk swim in a freezing waterhole to ease aching muscles and invigorate you for your next day's exploration.

Some rides, such as the intimate treks out of The Willows, cater exclusively for experienced riders who are confident with long hours in the saddle and an unstructured route. The less experienced riders may prefer to join a larger, more commercial group – Reynella, for instance, a company based near Adaminaby in NSW, caters

LEFT *At the foothills of the mountains, gentle farmland shaded by magnificent eucalyptus trees makes superb riding terrain.*

for all standards with their popular treks into the northern realms of the Kosciuszko National Park. Even absolute beginners are welcome, and it's fantastic to see reticent and nervous riders begging for more at the end of a five-day ride.

Reynella is one of the few NSW horse-riding organizations that has permission to take its clients on rides in the national parks. A six-day trek usually covers around 160km (99 miles), based around a campsite at Tantangara Dam near Lake Eucumbene. The daily route is dependent on weather, riders' ability and sheer whim, covering locations such as Cave Creek, Currango Plain and Mount Morgan. Most rides set off in the cool of early morning, when the grass is dewy and shadows long; by lunchtime, weary riders and horses take a welcome break, indulging in packed sandwiches, fruit cake and

delicious billy tea, flavoured with the essences of the Australian bush. Rustic cattleman's huts, historic vestiges of the pioneer era, are favoured resting points; grassy riverbanks are another welcome sight, with a skinny dip often in order. Cooled and refreshed, riders mount for another three-hour stint. As the sun dips over the mountains and the peaks turn from lavender to orange to vermilion, riders delight in the wonders of the Australian bush as 'roos', wallabies and wild horses venture out to graze.

After six bone-crunching hours in the saddle, the evening camp is a welcome sight. Weary

---

ABOVE *Decked out in traditional oilskin Driza-Bones®, a riding group sets out through a typical rural landscape.*

horses, unsaddled and washed down, head for the nearest sandy patch for a limb-stretching roll; while riders limp off to bathe or to drink a few 'tinnies' of beer. Thereafter, the Australian night engulfs and soothes, with starry skies and the eerie sounds of nocturnal marsupials to entertain and intrigue.

Here, with campfire embers softly glowing, the soothing strum of a guitar, and the gentle stomp of a horse's hoof, you experience peace in its purest form. It's an unparalleled experience, one that invigorates every fibre of your body, from your recharged brain to your aching body. It is, perhaps, the ultimate escape from the stresses of modern city living and 21st-century mania – a physical and spiritual journey into one of the most remote, ancient wildernesses in the world.

Hurunui Backcountry Adventure

*H*urunui Backcountry Adventure
CANTERBURY REGION, NEW ZEALAND

Location *Hurunui, South Island*

Getting there *Less than two hours drive from*
Christchurch Airport

Season *October–April*

Duration *¹/₂ day to 10-day rides*

Group size *Maximum of 8 riders; maximum*
of 4 for 'Station to Station' ride

Horses *Station hack, Connemara*

Tack *English; Western; stock saddles*

Pace *Moderate*

Riding ability *All riders welcome, some*
experience preferred

'Every day we went there, spirits rose, whether it had snowed overnight, or the sun was out or it was pelting rain. There was majesty to that location. A secret valley, it seemed. A place where, if it had not been for the film, one would never have visited. That was a really magical time…'
SIR IAN MCKELLEN, actor, THE LORD OF THE RINGS

Apart from all the gorgeous and talented stars of Peter Jackson's movie adaptation of *The Lord the Rings*, the most breathtaking feature was the scenery of New Zealand. Film-goers gasped at the towering snowcapped mountains, the endless alpine vistas and the glistening, azure lakes; and the questions were asked – where is this beautiful place, does it really exist, and can I go there? Suddenly, this insignificant island nation at the tail end of the Pacific Ocean had revealed itself as a mountain paradise far from the turmoil of the modern world.

As Gandalf, played by Sir Ian McKellen, rode towards Edoras, a hillside town purpose-built on a high country sheep station in the Canterbury region of the South Island, one thing certainly became apparent to equine-loving film viewers – this indeed is horse heaven; the landscape crying out for the creak of leather, the jingle of a bit and the pounding of hooves on a long, hard gallop.

Of course, this is no secret to the locals. In its short modern history, New Zealand has become synonymous with horses – Phar Lap, Australasia's most revered racehorse was born and bred here. New Zealand-bred horses continue to dominate the multimillion-dollar racing industry in the Southern Hemisphere and beyond.

Since 1814, when the controversial evangelist Samuel Marsden first transported horses across the Tasman Sea, a strong horse culture has developed in New Zealand, with extensive participation in eventing, show-jumping, hunting and pony clubs as well as the racing scene.

Until recently, the horse was also widely used in agricultural activities, the rugged terrain negating the use of four-wheeled vehicles. Farmers needed strong, surefooted animals that could handle the steep hills and rocky river beds, as well as survive the chilly winters on minimal feed. Thoroughbreds, while beloved by the locals, are not the hardiest of creatures; so the station-bred stock horses were often crossbreeds, combining the beauty and stance of the Thoroughbred with the sturdiness of the heavier Clydesdale or cob breeds favoured for farming.

The result was a tough, general-purpose mount that was tall and strong, known as 'station hacks'. They generally make excellent hunters, bold and forward going with enormous jumps – they'll even take on wire fences during the popular winter fox hunts!

It is in the backcountry of the South Island that these sturdy riding horses come into their own. *Lord of the Rings* may portray what looks like a horsy paradise, but the altitude, rocky ground and inclement climate of the Southern Alps all take their toll on lesser beasts. A station hack working the New Zealand High Country needs to be fit, surefooted, level-headed and an excellent doer. Quality station horses and a practical approach to horsemanship are the trademarks

LEFT *A guide leads a packhorse cross Hurunui River, one of the many crossings which challenges horse and rider alike.*

OPPOSITE *Trek horses pick their way through a beech forest, which is one of the few uncleared pockets in this agricultural landscape.*

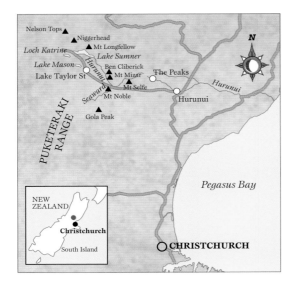

established, with an emphasis on good, honest hard work. Guests are encouraged to participate in the infrastructure of the ride, from pitching tents and cooking meals to grooming and saddling the horses – involvement is the key to a group dynamic and the subsequent camaraderie experienced on the rides. It's not unusual to find people from vastly different backgrounds enjoying each other's company, having nothing in common except a love of horses and the great outdoors. I found that there's nothing quite like a trek on horseback as a social equalizer.

One thing that is likely to confound all and sundry, whether a high-ranking businessman, American university student or Cockney chef, is the workings of a packsaddle! This is a challenge that most clients relish, a skill they never thought they'd attempt or need, and a fascinating feature of the wilderness treks. Rides without vehicle support are accompanied by at least two packhorses carrying swags, luggage and supplies for the duration of the trip. Putting the complicated harness on is difficult enough; but even more challenging is packing the saddle bags, which must be of equal weight and bulk for the horses to carry them comfortably .

The pace of the rides is largely dictated by the packhorses – it's difficult to have a long canter when the supplies are at risk. Riders on packhorse treks, such as the four-day Seaward River trip, should expect a steady pace with a lot of walking, only occasionally breaking into a faster trot or canter.

The focus of most of the Hurunui rides is the sheep stations in the Lake Sumner region. The mountains of the Southern Alps, bearing evocative names such as Mt Noble, Mt Longfellow, Ben Cliberick and Phyllis Fell, circle this beautiful high country lake. Rivers bubbling at the foot of the peaks are fuelled by glacial run-off – the Waitohi, the Seaward and

of one of New Zealand's premier horse-riding organizations, Hurunui Horse Treks. These rides are based at Mandy Platt and Rob Stanley's peaceful rural enclave, The Peaks, located an hour's drive from Christchurch on the green patchwork of the Canterbury Plains. Halfway between the city and the thermal resort of Hanmer Springs, this is a convenient and accessible location for international visitors, many of whom extend their New Zealand riding vacation with further exploration of the majestic Alpine region.

Physically demanding and visually stimulating, an extended trek into this beautiful part of the South Island certainly satisfies and stimulates every sense. Around every corner and over every hill there is a delightful surprise – spectacular vistas of the Southern Alps; a farmer working his sheep; steep river gorges shrouded in afternoon shade; or the magic of a mysterious beech forest abuzz with the hum of wasps.

These are scenes hidden from most tourists' eyes. The treks take place largely on private property, or on public trails inaccessible to vehicles, so riders really can experience a local perspective. A human presence is limited in this remote landscape – a group may ride all day and only encounter the odd farmer or hunter, more intent on tracking their prey than engaging in light-hearted conversation.

From the moment of arrival at The Peaks, the down-to-earth and no-nonsense tone is clearly

ABOVE RIGHT *A group of horse riders pause to contemplate the magnificent highland scenery of North Canterbury, recalling scenes from* The Lord of the Rings.

the blue Hurunui rivers are all perfect locations for a lunchtime break and an afternoon swim.

The most challenging of the Hurunui rides is the 'Mountains to the Sea', an eight-day pack trip which traverses remote country between Hanmer Springs and Kaikoura, a beautiful fishing village famed for its superlative whale and

dolphin watching. This is an adventure in the truest sense, crossing some of the hardest country in New Zealand. There are no luxuries on this trek – riders must be prepared to sleep rough, and travel light. The days are long, the river crossings perilous, and the presence of heavily laden packhorses keeps the pace slow and steady. This is a ride for people who are comfortable in the saddle and know how to look after themselves and their horses. Riders are expected to be fit, hardworking and the willingness to participate is mandatory. It is not a ride for passengers, but genuine 'horse' people with a pioneering spirit.

Heading off from the alpine spa resort, the ride crosses the Hanmer Range at Jollies Pass and fords the mighty Clarence River before entering Molesworth Station, the biggest sheep station in New Zealand. Here, the land becomes drier and less hospitable; the land is stark and broken, making it tough going for the horses.

camp in their fields or overnight in shearers' quarters or woolsheds. A home-cooked country breakfast is the perfect start to a full day in the saddle, while evening get-togethers involve a hearty meal, some genuine rural hospitality, studying of maps and involved discussions about the price of wool and the merits of mutton – conversations you'll only ever have in New Zealand!

As you study the intricacies of the topographical maps with their indecipherable swirls and lines, you suddenly become aware of how insignificant and localized the ground you are covering really is. Six hours in the saddle may amount to only 15km (9 miles) in total, taking into account the challenging elevation and rough terrain. And with every breathtaking ascent up a tussock ridge, there is an equally challenging descent, with riders dismounting to ease the burden on their mounts and stretch their own weary legs.

Tapuae-o-Uenuku, the highest point outside the Southern Alps, is a prominent landmark.

After a night's accommodation at the historic Molesworth Station, the ride heads east to cross the rugged Seaward Kaikoura Range. After days in the mountains, the sight of the blue Pacific

Ocean is a song for the soul – spirits lift at the magnificent sight, which is a welcome reward after such a long and challenging ride.

A special feature of the Hurunui backcountry treks is the opportunity to share meals with local farmers who generously allow riders to

One of the biggest challenges on all the Hurunui rides is river crossing. Huge boulders and swirling, icy waters make uneasy footing for the unshod horses that are forced to pick their way through, finding their own path to avoid slipping into crevices. Riders are advised to drop their stirrups and rely 100 per cent on their steed's intuition and common sense. Should the horse stumble and fall, at least the riders can escape easily and safely, an embarrassing dunking hopefully being the only aftermath!

One of the great pleasures during a summer ride, however, is swimming the horses through the waist-high channels; simply drop your stirrups, hang onto the mane and let your pony do the hard work.

Another unique reward on longer treks is a soak in a natural thermal pool, secluded amid beech forest. These thermal waters originate

ABOVE LEFT *A group of horse trekkers slowly ascends further into the mountains of New Zealand's Hurunui backcountry.*

LEFT *Hanmer Springs thermal pools are the ideal place to soak and relax after a long horseback ride through the backcountry.*

from rainwater seeping down through rock fractures caused by seismic activity – heat radiating from the earth's core then raises the temperature of the water and forces it back to the surface in the form of hot springs. This whole process takes a long time – the water in the pools may have fallen as rain more than 100 years ago. There's nothing quite like a soak in a 40°C (104°F) pool of water to wash away the aches and pains of

hours in the saddle. The springs are also a great place to warm up: once the sun starts to drop, so does the temperature, with chilly evenings even in the middle of summer. It's little wonder that

ABOVE *The use of a packhorse, combined with the rugged terrain, restricts riders to a steady pace during a Hurunui horse trek.*

the Maori, originally from balmier climes further north in the Pacific, spent much of their time in the thermal pools, exploiting its warmth for cooking, bathing and good health.

The therapeutic benefits of thermal pools are now well documented. Less well known are the refreshing and healing qualities of riding in New Zealand. If someone could bottle that enriching experience, he would soon become a millionaire!

Appendix: Booking & General Information

THE AMERICAS

Canada
Warner Guiding & Outfitting Ltd
1 Sundance Road, Banff, Alberta
Tel: +1-403-762-4551
Fax: +1-403-762-8130
e-mail: warner@horseback.com
Website: www.horseback.com

USA
Bitterroot Ranch
1480 East Fork Road, Dubois
WY 82513
Wyoming
Tel: +1-307-455-3363
Fax: +1-307-455-2354
e-mail: bitterroot@wyoming.com
Website: www.bitterroot.com

Mexico
Finca Enyhe
Calle de Tierras Blancas 363
Barrio de Otumba, Valle de Bravo
Edo. Mex. C.P. 51200
Tel/fax: +52-726-262-0636
e-mail:
info@mexicohorsevacation.com
Website:
www.mexicohorsevacation.com

Costa Rica
Costa Rican Horse Adventures
Casa 2, Residencial Robledal
125 mts Sur de Abonos
Agro, La Uruca, San José
Tel: +506-520-0346
Fax: +506-520-0323
e-mail:
info@costaricanhorseadventures.com
Website:
www.costaricanhorseadventures.com

Chile
Via Equitrek (see Agents listings)

Iceland
Eldhestar
Vellir Ölfusi, Box 90
810 Hveragerdi
Tel: +354-480-4800
Fax: +354-480-4801
e-mail: info@eldhestar.is
Website: www.eldhestar.is

EUROPE

Ireland
Via Equitrek (see Agents listings)

Scotland
Argyll Trail Riding
Brenfield Farm, Ardrishaig
Argyll, PA30 8ER
Tel: +44-1546-603-274
Fax: +44-1546-603-225
e-mail: info@brenfield.co.uk
Website: www.brenfield.co.uk

England
D&P Equestrian Enterprises
Low Haygarth Farm, Cautley
Sedbergh
Cumbria, LA 10 5NE
Tel/fax: +44-0-1539-620-349
e-mail:
barbara@dandpequestrian.co.uk
Website:
www.dandpequestrian.co.uk

France
Via World Horse Riding
(see Agents listings)

Spain
Los Alamos Equestrian Holidays
La Canada del Alamo, Canos de
Mecca, Barbate, Cadiz
Tel/fax: +34-956-437-416
e-mail:
andrew@losalamosriding.co.uk
Website:
www.losalamosriding.co.uk

Italy
Agriturismo Malvarina
Country Inn Malvarina
Tel/fax: +39-075-806-4280
e-mail: info@malvarina.it
Website: www.malvarina.it

Hungary
Lehner Major
8716 Gadány
Hungary
Tel: +36-30-226-9553
Fax: +36-85-337-053
e-mail: riding@hunyady.hu
Website: www.hunyady.hu

Turkey
Akhal-Teke Horse Center
Aydin Alti Mah, Gesteric Sok 21
Avanos 50500, Nevsehir
Turkiye
Tel: +90-384-511-5171
Fax: +90-384-511-3370
e-mail:
mail@akhal-tekehorsecenter.com
Website:
www.akhal-tekehorsecenter.com

AFRICA

South Africa
Equus Horse Safaris
Vaalwater 0530
South Africa
Tel: +27-14-721-0063
Fax +27-14-721-0062
e-mail: equus@equus.co.za
Website: www.equus.co.za

Horizon Horseback Adventures &
Saddlebag Safaris
Triple B Ranch, Vaalwater
Waterberg
Tel: +27-14-755-4003
Fax: +27-14-755-4418
e-mail: horizonranch@yebo.co.za
Websites: www.ridinginafrica.com

Botswana
Okavango Horse Safaris
Quanticon Offices, Tau Street
Boseja
Maun
Tel: +267-686-1671
Fax: +267-686-1672
e-mail: ohsnx@info.bw
Website: www.okavangohorse.com

Kenya
Offbeat Safaris Ltd
Deloraine Estate, Nairobi
Tel: +254-051-32005
Fax: +254-051-343122/3
e-mail: offbeat@africaonline.co.ke
Website: www.offbeatsafaris.com

ASIA

India
Royal Equestrian and Polo Centre
Dundlod, Shekhawati
Tel: +91-141-221-1276
Fax: +91-141-221-1498
e-mail: dundlod@datainfosys.net
Website: www.dundlod.com

Mongolia
Karakorum Expeditions Mongolia
Gangariin Gurav Bld, 1st Floor
(SW side of State Circus), Ulaanbaatar
Tel/fax: +976-11-315-655
e-mail: info@GoMongolia.com
Website: www.GoMongolia.com

AUSTRALIA AND NEW ZEALAND

Australia
The Willows
Anglers Rest, Victoria
Tel: +61-3-5159-6445
e-mail: mrsed@tpg.com.au
Website:
www.dinnerplaintrailrides.com

Reynella Kosciuszko Rides
Adaminaby, NSW 2630
Tel: +61-2-6454-2386
Fax: +61-2-6454-2530
e-mail: reynella@snowy.net.au
Web: www.reynellarides.com.au

New Zealand
Ridenz
Ribbonwood, Hawarden RD1
North Canterbury
Tel/fax: +64-3-314-4204
e-mail: info@ridenz.com
Website: www.ridenz.com

AGENTS

Hidden Trails
202–380 West 1 Avenue
Vancouver, BC V5Y 3T7
Tel: 604-323-1141
Fax: 604-323-1148
e-mail: outdoor@hiddentrails.com
Website: www.hiddentrails.com

In the Saddle
Reaside, Neen Savage, Cleobury
Mortimer, Shropshire, DY14 8ES
United Kingdom
Tel: +44-0-1299-272-997
Fax: +44-0-1299-272-935
e-mail: rides@inthesaddle.com
Website: www.inthesaddle.com

Equitrek Australia
Contact: Nelly Gelich
Tel: +61-2-9913-9408
Fax: +61-2-9970-6303
e-mail: ride@equitrek.com.au
Website: www.equitrek.com.au

Equitour UK
The Bell
Church Street, Charlbury
Oxford
England
OX3PP
Tel: +44-0-1608-819182
Fax: +44-0-1608-811447
e-mail: louise@equitour.co.uk
Website: www.equitour.co.uk

Ride World Wide
Staddon Farm, North Tawton
Devon EX20 2BX
United Kingdom
Tel: +44-0-1837-8544
Fax: +44-0-1837-8179
e-mail: RideWW@aol.com
Website: www.rideworldwide.com

Unicorn Trails
2 Acorn Centre, Chestnut Avenue
Biggleswade, Beds, SG18 ORA
United Kingdom
Tel: +44-0-1767-600-606
Fax: +44-0-1767-312-555
e-mail: info@unicorntrails.com
Website: www.unicorntrails.com

World Horse Riding
Contact: Anna Widstrand
Östra Vallgatan 57
SE-223 61 Lund
Sweden
Tel: +46-046-152-291
Fax: +46-046-152-291

or:
Via Bernardino Butinone 3
IT-24047 Treviglio (BG)
Italy
Tel: +39-0363-301-434
Fax: +39-0363-301-434
e-mail:
anna@worldhorseriding.com
Website:www.worldhorseriding.com

KEY TO PHOTOGRAPHERS

Copyright rests with the following photographers and/or their agents.
Key to Locations: t = top; tl = top left; tc = top centre; tr = top right; b = bottom; bl = bottom left; bc = bottom centre; br = bottom right; l = left; r = right; c = centre. (*No abbreviation is given for pages with a single image, or pages on which all photographs are by same the photographer.*)

Photographers:
AAWTL = AA World Travel Library
AB = Arnd Bronkhorst
AS = Adrian Summers
APL = Australian Picture Library
BBC = British Broadcasting Corporation
   (SW = Staffan Widstrand)
BF = Barry Ferguson
BL = Bob Langrish
DH = Dennis Hardley
FB = Franco Barbagallo

FE = Finca Enyhe
GB = Gabriele Boiselle
HH = Hedgehog House
   (CM = Colin Monteath)
HHT = Hurunui Horse Treks
HT = Hidden Trails
JM = Jill Malcolm
JulM = Julie Miller
JW = Jasper Winn
KH = Kit Houghton
KS = Kevin Schafer

P & BP = Peter & Beverly Pickford
PA = Photo Access (CL = C Lanz;
   DB = Dave Bristow)
PH = Paul Harris
RD = Robyn Daly
RWW = Ride World Wide
SC = Sue Cunningham
SV = Scottish Viewpoint
   (PT = Paul Tomkins)
VE = Victor Englebert

Page	Loc	Photographer
Front cover		P & BP
Back cover		GB
Spine		PH
Endpapers		RD
1		AS
2–3		JW
4–5		KH
6–7		PA/CL
8	tl	AS
8	bl	PA/CL
9		PH
10–11		KH
12–13		GB
14		BF
15		BL
16–17		BF
18	tl	BF
18	br	JulM
19		JulM
20		GB
21		GB
22–23		KH
24–25		JulM
26	l	JulM
26–27		KH
28		HT
29–30		RWW
31–32		FE
33		HT
34		AAWTL
35–36		SC
37	t	VE
37	b	SC
38	t	KS
38	b	SC
39	tr	AAWTL
39	bl	KS
40		JW
41–42		PH
43		JW
44	t	BBC/SW
44	bl	JulM
45		AAWTL
46–47		AAWTL
48–53		GB
54		AB
55		GB
56–57		AAWTL
58		GB
59		AAWTL
60		JulM
61–63		SV/PT
63	r	DH
64	tl	JulM
64	br	SV
65		AAWTL
66		KH
67		BL
68–74		KH
75–77		GB
78–79		BL
79	bl	KH
80–88		GB
89		BL
90–112		GB
113–114		PA/CL
115		FB
116		GB
117		PA/DB
118–119		GB
120–121		RD
122–127		GB
128–129		AS
130–131		GB
132–135		KH
136–141		AS
142–145		KH
146–147		APL
148–149		KH
150		JM
151		JulM
152–153		AAWTL
154	tl	HHT
154	bl	HH/CM
155		AAWTL
160		GB

Index

Figures in bold indicate that the entries appear in photographs

*A*brivado fiesta **75**
Adams, Wendy 114, 115
Africa 108–127
Agritourismo 90
airak 141
Akhal-Teke Horse **102**, 104, 105
Akhal-Teke Riding Center 104, 105
Alpine National Park 148
Altai Mountains **8**, **137**, **139**, 140
American Quarter Horse 82
Americas, The 12–45
Andalucian 80 *see also Pura Raza Española*
Andalucian Horse 36, 85, 80, **82**
Anglers Rest 148
Anglo-Arab 113
Anhold, Tilman 57
Appendex 31
Arabs **26–27**, 36
Aravilli Hills 135
Arenal Lake **37**
Argyll Trail Riding 60
Asia 128–141
Australia 144–149
Australia and New Zealand 142–155
Australian Stock Horse 140, 146
Avanos 105, **106**
*B*allycormac House 54
Banff National Park 14, **15**, 16
baqueno 40, 42, **43**, **45**
Bardamat Hills 126
Ben Bulben 56
Ben Cliberick 152
Ben Nevis 65
Bestelink, Barney 116, 120
Bestelink, PJ 116, 120
Bitterroot **12–13**, **22–23**
black bulls **76**, **77**
Blue Duck Inn, The 148
Boerperd **110**, 113, 115
Bogong High Plains 148

Botswana 116–121
Brenfield Farm 60
Brontë sisters 68
brumbies **146–147**
Buachille Etive Beag 65
bull elk **18**
Bundarrah River 148
Burton, Barbara 69
*C*amargue **46–47**
Camargue Horse **74**, 77, **78**
Canada 14–19
Cape Horse 115
Cape Trafalgar **84**, 86, 87
Cappodocia Highlight tour 106
Cassidy, Butch 23
Castle Riding Centre 60
cattle drive **25**
Cave Creek 149
charro 31, 33
Chile 40–45
Church of the Buckle 106 *see also Tokali Kilise*
Church, Tony 124
Clifford, Lady Anne 72
Cloud Forests 38
Coast of Light 84 *see also Costa de la Luz*
Connemara Pony **58**
Continental Divide 23, 38
Costa de la Luz **84** *see also Coast of Light*
Costa Rica 34–39
Costa Rican Criollo 36, 39
Cotswold 66, **67**
Craig's Hut 148
Criollos 31, 32, 40
Crystal, Billy 20
csikós **94**, **95**, **97**, **99**
Cuarros River 37
Cuernos (Horns) del Paine 43
Cumbria **66**, **68**
*D*efoe, Daniel 64
Dernish Isle 57
Dickson Glacier 43, 44
Dilari, Ercihan 105

Donegal Bay **54**, 56
Dowinton, Shane 113
Driza-Bones ® 146, **149**
Dry Central Pacific Region 37
dude ranch 20
Dundlod Fort **132**, 135
Duntrane Castle 64
*E*co-tourism 34
El Campo 87
El Hoyo 32
El Palmar 86
Eldhestar 52
Elves Church 52
Emerald Isle 54
England 66–73
Epona Riding Centre 84
Equus 114, **115**
Estancia Terrecera 44
Europe 46–107
*F*abrizi, Claudio 90, 91
Fabrizi, Patrizia 90
Fairy Chimneys **103**, 106
Falls Creek 148
Fat Lamb Country Inn 69
Finca Enyhe 28, **33**
Flints Peak 18
Fox, Bayard 22, **26**, 126, 127
Fox, Mel 26
Framan, Judie 54
France 74–79
frog, red-eyed tree **38**
*G*ardian **75**, 76, 78, **79**
geldings 18
Gelich, Nelly 8, 59
Genghis Khan's Golden Horde 138
ger **138**, 140, 141
Geysir 53
Giantess Waterfall 53 *see also Trollkonuhlaup*
Glen Coe 65
Glen Kinglass 65
Glen Shira 65
Glen Valley 148
Golden Falls, The 53 *see also Gullfoss*

Golden Highlights of the South 52
Göreme Open Air Museum 106
Gorkhi Terelj National Park 141
Gray-Stephens, Tove 60
Guanacaste National Park 39
guanacos **43**
Gullfoss 53 *see also* Golden Falls
*H*acienda La Maravilla 37
Hanmer Springs 152, **154**
Hartley Castle 72
havelis 135
Hay-Thorburn, David **60**, 62, 63
Healy Creek **16**
Hell's Window 148
helmets 10
Herriot, James 68
Horse Holiday Farm 56, 57, 59
Horse Riding Ireland 54
Hosteria Mirador Del Payne 44
Howgill Fells 69
Hungarian Warmblood **96**, 97
Hungary 94–101
Hurunui **154**
Hurunui River **150**
I Sentieri del Tempo 91 *see also* Paths of Light, The
Iceland 48–53
Icelandic Horse **48**, **50**, **52**, **53**
India 130–135
Inverary Castle **65**
Irazú volcano **34**
Ireland 54–59
Irish Cob 64
Irish Draught 57
Italy 88–93
*K*enya 122–127
Khan Khentii Protected Area 141
Khan, Genghis 141
Kharkhiraa mountains **128–129**, **140**
Khovsgol Nuur 140, **141**
Kizilirmak river 105 *see also* Red River
Kosciuszko National Park 144, 149
Kransberg peaks 114 115

La Sierra Cavalcade 28, 33
Lago Dickson **44**
Lago Nordenskjold 45
Lago Pingo **40**
Lago Sarmiento 45
Laguna Azul 40, **42** *see also*
   Lake Azul
Lake Azul 42 *see also* Luguna Azul
Lake Eucumbene 149
Lake Louise 14
Lake Sumner 152
Lakes District 66, 69
Lapalala Wilderness **114**
Le Trec 62 *see also Techniques de*
   Randonner Equestrien de Compétition
Les Saintes Maries de la Mer 79
Lesotho 110
l'Étang du Fangassier 78
Liota Hills 125
Loch and Forest Trail **61**, 62
Loch Etive 65
Loch Fyne 62, **64**
Los Alamos 85, 87
Los Canos de Meca 85, 87
Los Innocente Hacienda 39
Los Tres Reyes 32 *see also*
   three kings, The
Lough Gill **59**
Low Haygarth Farm 69, 71
Maasai tribesman **123**, 125
Macateers Camp **117**
Magyars **94**
Mallerstang Valley 72
malopo channels **118–119**
Malvarina 90, 93
manyattas 125
Mara River 126
Marakele National Park 115
mariachi 28
Marsden, Samuel 150
Marwari Horse **130**, 132, **135**
Masai Mara National Park **122**,
   124, **125**
maté 42, 43
Maurillo, Maria 90, 93
McKellen, Sir Ian 150
Mexico 28–33
Mhairi **60**, 64

Molesworth Station 154
Monarch Butterfly Sanctuary 33
Mongolia 136–141
Mongolian Horse **1**
Monte Alto 32
Monteverde Cloud Forest 38, **39**
Moremi Game Reserve 118
Mount Erciyes 102
Mount Hotham 148
Mount Kosciuszko 146
Mount Longfellow 152
Mount Morgan 149
Mount Noble 152
Mount Sabasio 90, 92, 93
mules **14**, 16, 18, 19, 32
Musgrave, Sir Richard 72
Mystic Camp 18
Naguar Fair 135
New Zealand **10**, 150–155
North Canterbury **152–153**
Odyssey tour 37, 38, 39
Okavango Delta 112, **116**, 119, 120
orchid, sobralia **39**
Palomino, Paloma 33
Parque Naturel de la
   Breña y Las Marismas 86
Paterson, Banjo 144
Paths of Light, The 91 *see also*
   I Sentieri del Tempo
Peaks, The 152
Pendragon Castle 71
Pennines **2–3**
Peruvian Pasos 36, 82
Phar Lap Horse 150
Platt, Mandy 152
Priestley, JB 72
Przewalski Horse 140
Punta Arenas 40, 42
Pura Raza Española 80 *see also*
   Andalucian
Pushkar Camel Fair **135**
puszta 94
Pyrénées 76
Questo 45
Rainbow Lake 14, **16**
Rajasthan **11**, 135
randonnée liberté 76
raseteurs 79

Red River 105 *see also*
   Kizilirmak River
refugio 44
Reykjavík 48, 52
Ring of Kerry 54
River Add 64
River Eden 72
River Orchy 65
River Rhône 74
Rob Roy Trail 62, 65
Roy, Rob 60, 62, 64, 65
Royal Andalucian School of
   Equestrian Art 84
Royal Equestrian and Polo Centre 132
Sabanero 36
Schravesande, José (Pepe) 28, 31
Schravesande, Lucia **28**, 31
Scotland 60–65
Scott, Lord Francis 124
Scott, Sir Walter 65
Seaward Kaikoura Range 154
Semel, Wendy A 87
sentiers de grande randonnée 76
Shekhawati 132, 135
Shoshone National Park **21**, 23
Sierra del Torro **45**
Sierra Navada 83
Singh, Kanwar Raghuvendra 132
Smardale Nature Reserve 71
Smith, Di 92
Snowy Mountains 8, **142–143**, 146
Snowy River 146
Somogy 98, **100**, **101**
Somogy County Provincial Association
   for Nature Conservation 98, 99
South Africa 110–115
Spain 80–87
Stanley, Rob 152
station hacks 150
Stoney Camp 18
Strokkur 53
Sulphur Mountain 14, 17
Tack room **31**
Techniques de Randonner Equestrien
   de Compétition 62 *see also* Le Trec
Thjófafoss 53 *see also*
   Waterfall of Thieves
Thoroughbred 113

Three Kings, The 32 *see also*
   Los Tres Reyes
tico 34, **37**
Tilaran Mountains 38
Tokali Kilise 106 *see also*
   Church of the Buckle
tölt 51
Torres del Paine 40
Torres del Tajo 87
Traveler **26**
Triple B Ranch 113
Trollafoss 52 *see also*
   Troll-Woman's Waterfall
Trollkonuhlaup 53 *see also*
   Giantess Waterfall
Troll-Woman's Waterfall 52 *see*
   also Trollafoss
tufa 102, 106
Turkey 102--107
Uçhisar 106
Ulaanbaatar 140
Umbria 88
UNESCO Waterberg Biosphere
   Reserve 115
Ürgüp 106
USA 20–27
Valle de Bravo 28, **32**
vaquero 28
Victorian High Country 146
Voorspuy, Tristan 124, 126
Walker, Clive 110
Waterberg wilderness **6–7,8**
Waterfall of Thieves 52 *see*
   also Thjófafoss
Welsh Cobs 69
Wicklow Trail 54
Widstrand, Anna 78
Wild Boar Fell 72
Wild Boar Trail 62, 64, 71
Willows, The 148
Wind River 23
World Horse Riding 78
Wyoming **4–5**
Xenophon 80
Xudum river system 118
Yeats, William Butler 56, 57
Yellowstone Park 23
Yorkshire Dales 68, 69, **70–71**

'No hour of life is wasted that is spent in the saddle'
Sir Winston Churchill

Acknowledgements

Putting together a project of this magnitude is time and labour intensive. Firstly, thanks to the airlines and tourism bodies that assisted my passage – South African Airways, United Airlines, Tourism New Zealand, Wyoming Tourism, Alberta Tourism and IJ Singh.

Thanks to Bonnie Singh, Laura and Shane Dowinton, Wendy Adams, Barney & PJ, Mandy & Rob Platt, Warner Guiding and Outfitting, Bayard and Mel Fox, Roz and John Rudd and Helen Packer for sharing their patches of horsy heaven with me.

To the various horse-riding agents who offered advice – I couldn't have done it without you. Also Ruth Staines, Judie Framan, Karen Stahl, Paloma Palomino, Wendy A Semel, John Ruler, Anna Widstrand, Graham Taylor and Di Smith thank you for your contributions.

Big thank you to the team at New Holland, especially my dedicated and sensitive editors, Alfred LeMaitre and Leizel Brown.

To Nelly – my inspiration, friend and co-contributor – thanks for being such a trouper! To Tara and Sporty, a prince among horses – for teaching me to stay high in the saddle! Mum, Jules and Jaya – thanks for holding the fort and feeding the cat. And of course, love always to Simon and Jo for indulging my ridiculous passion.

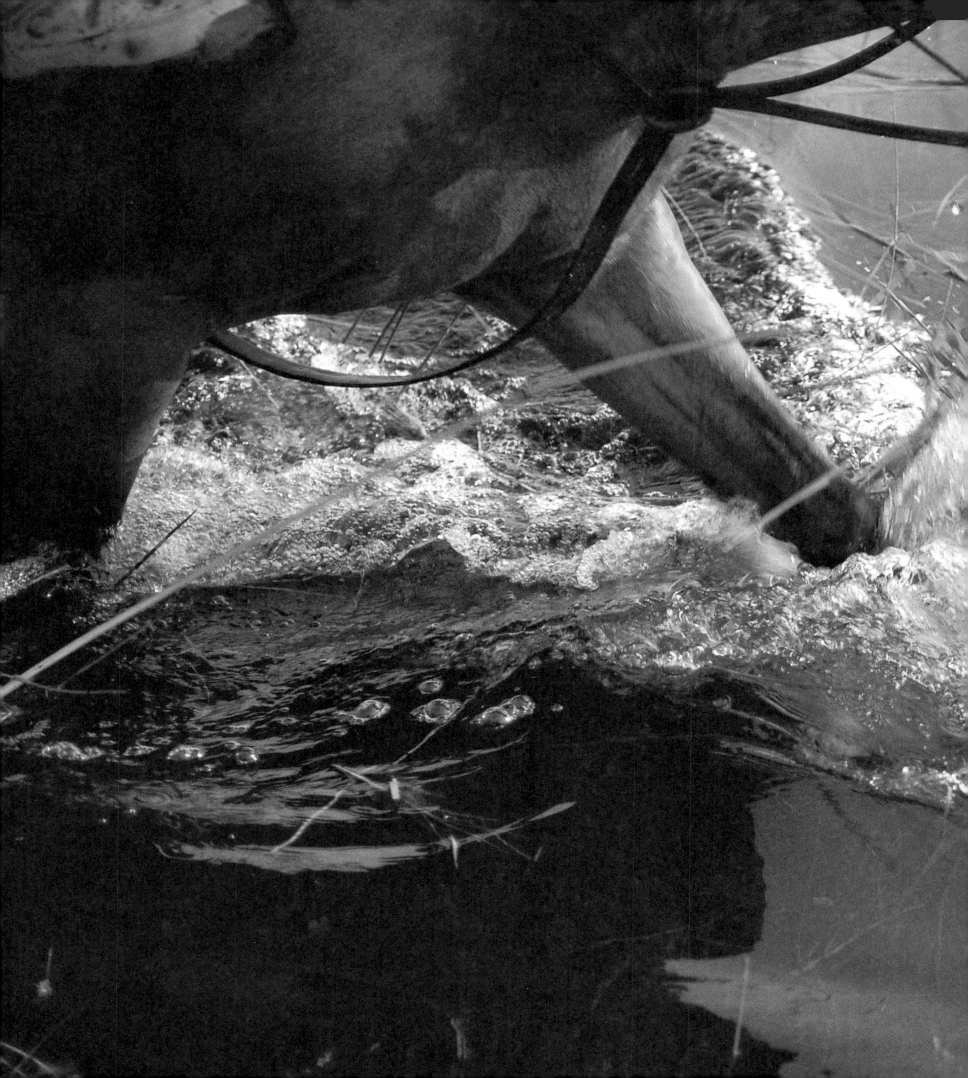